Tying and Fishing Southern Appalachian Trout Flies

Don Howell

with contributions from Kevin Howell

A Fern Creek Press Southern Appalachian Guidebook

Tying and Fishing Southern Appalachian Trout Flies

by Don Howell
Illustrations by John Brinkley - Pisgah Forest, North Carolina
Flies tied by Kevin Howell

ISBN #1-893651-02-9
Published by Fern Creek Press
P.O. Box 1322
Clayton, GA 30525
(706) 782-5379

Printed by Vaughan Printing, Nashville, Tennessee.

Contents

Tying and Fishing Southern Appalachian Trout Flies

Dwight Howell (l) and Don Ray Howell.
Photo taken in 1991 by Debbie Chase Jennings of the Asheville Citizen Times.

Dedication

This book is dedicated to my children - Kevin, Zane, and Kendra, and to the memory of my brother, Dwight, and my father, Don, who always had the time and patience to teach me how to fish and respect my environment.

- Don Ray Howell

Fly Fishing Memories

It's true! God does smile upon a few chosen people. God has given me the ability to understand the concept of fishing, blessed me with the health to fish, and allowed me to live in an area that not only has a lot of trout, but a lot of trophy trout. God has also provided me with a job that is conducive to a great deal of fishing, and He has given me the love and support of a wonderful family that encourages my love, dedication, and addiction to the sport.

My introduction to trout fishing came early in life. So early, in fact, that I can't remember going on my first fishing trip or catching my first trout. My family delights in telling the story of how my father would take my brother, Dwight, and me trout fishing when we were so small that he had to carry us on his back while wading and fishing.

On one of our trips, Dad hooked an extremely large trout. As usual, Dwight was riding on Dad's back and became very excited upon realizing the size of the fish. In his excitement, Dwight threw his hands over Dad's eyes and began yelling, "Get him out, Dad! Get him out, Dad!" Needless to say, Dad never landed the trout, and I can never remember Dad being upset with Dwight for costing him a trophy. Normally, Dad was more interested in making sure that Dwight and I had an enjoyable trip, and that we learned to have respect for our quarry and the environment.

My introduction to trout fishing was on the Linville River in Avery County, North Carolina. During my early years of trout fishing, Linville was one of the most insect rich and productive trout streams in eastern America, and possibly in the United States. The slow moving water, heavy hatches, and big, selective brown trout soon became an enjoyable classroom in which I learned many of my fishing techniques.

Through these experiences on Linville, I've been able to develop fly fishing techniques that have enabled me to take (and mostly release) over 350 trout that measured between twenty and thirty inches from public streams. Although I've been lucky enough to catch several large trout, I've never really considered myself an outstanding fisherman. I've certainly never felt that I possess the fishing or journalistic skills to write a book on the subject of trout fishing, although many of my fishing friends and family have constantly nagged at me to write a book.

It was the death of my father in July of 1992 that caused me to give consideration to the writing of this book. At the viewing of the body a friend of the family approached me and made the statement, "It's a shame that your father's knowledge of trout fishing can't be passed on. He has forgotten more about trout fishing than most people ever knew." I then realized that it was my obligation to share the many fishing techniques that Dad passed to me (along with the ones I developed during the forty-eight years we fished together) with others in the hope that they, too, will learn and enjoy the sport to its fullest extent. Many of the tactics discussed in this book are self-taught, and some may seem to be unorthodox, but they work - at least for me.

As indicated by the title, a portion of this book will be devoted to tying effective Southern Appalachian trout flies. Besides trout fishing, my first love is fly tying, and Dad was directly responsible for this interest. For you to understand how this interest was cultivated, it is necessary to know some of the history of my father.

At the age of six months, my dad, Don Daughtery Howell, fell out of a cradle into a fireplace and badly burned his left hand. Later, his fingers and a portion of his hand had to be amputated. Although his handicap did not prevent him from fly fishing, he was never able to tie flies.

Dad's favorite fly pattern was the Deer Hair, and at that time it was difficult to find a store that carried an ample supply. As a result, he often found himself with an empty fly box. Dad came up with the bright idea of buying fly tying kits for his sons - he would then have an endless supply of flies.

I received my kit at the age of eight and thus began my struggle learning to tie. At the time, there were very few tiers or books on fly tying. Dwight and I taught ourselves to tie by the trial-and-error method and for years the only equipment we had was a Herter's vise and scissors. I can remember trying to learn to tie the deer hair patterns by cutting strips of deer hair and wrapping it around the hook to form the irresistible body. Eventually, we learned to tie a respectable fly and I've tied commercially for the past thirty-five years. During this time, I've tied for Orvis, several shops in Tennessee, Montana, Wyoming, Alabama and North Carolina, as well as retailing my own flies.

This book will discuss tying methods for some of the more successful traditional patterns, but will concentrate mostly on modern patterns that have been developed by southern tiers. Hopefully, you will be able to incorporate many of these tying and fishing techniques into your fishing style and become a more successful fisherman.

Remember to release your catch. God smiles on those who allow other fishermen to use his precious resource more than once.

- Don Ray Howell

Part One

Southern Appalachian Trout Flies

Chapter One

"Yallar" Hammer Series

During the history of fly fishing, a few flies have been developed that seem to win the hearts of fishermen as well as the appetites of the trout. The "Yallar" Hammer developed a reputation in the Great Smoky Mountains and across the Southern Appalachians as strong as the national reputation of the Royal Wulff, Muddler Minnow, Adams, and Wooly Bugger.

The "Yallar" Hammer has played a large part in the history and development of fly fishing in the South, and I'm willing to bet my pet Sage Rod that there's not a serious trout fisherman in the Southern Appalachians that has not heard the legendary stories of the "Yallar" Hammer's ability to produce trout.

The "Yallar" Hammer was developed to catch speckled trout (brookies) in the streams that are now incorporated into the Great Smoky Mountains National Park. The fishermen in the area knew that brookies had a preference for brightly colored flies, but they were limited in the amount of brightly colored fly tying materials available due to the inferior dying methods of the time, a shortage of supply houses, and a shortage of money to purchase supplies. The local tiers were forced to rely upon natural, brightly colored materials.

Originally, the materials to tie the "Yallar" Hammer were taken from a woodpecker common to the Eastern United States. The woodpecker is known as a Flicker, Yellow-shafted Flicker, Golden-winged Woodpecker, High-holer, Yellow Hammer, or "Yallar" Hammer (the local pronunciation). The bird has a yellowish/black cast to its feathers and the primary wing feathers are prized material for forming bodies on all "Yallar" Hammer patterns. Unfortunately, the birds are an endangered species and it is illegal to have any feathers in your possession. There have been many attempts to imitate the pattern, but I've seen only one imitation that works as well as, and looks so much like, the original. This pattern is extremely difficult to distinguish from the true pattern.

The secret to tying this exact imitation is obtaining feathers that match the color, texture, and durability of the original. I've found only two birds that can be used (with special preparation) to meet these specifications: Mourning Doves and Bob White Quail. Fortunately, both of these are game birds, and you can enjoy the satisfaction of hunting them as well as tying flies from their feathers without violating existing game laws.

Preparation of the Feathers

As stated earlier, the secret to tying effective "Yallar" Hammer imitations is in securing and preparing the feathers. After you have obtained a supply of doves or quail (I prefer using quail, but both work nicely), clip the wing as close to the bird's body as possible and remove individual feathers from the wing. Wash them in warm water and mild detergent to remove any blood spots. Rinse the feathers in warm water, making sure all soap and oily residue is removed. If soap or oily residue is left on the feathers, they will not dye well.

Once the feathers have been clipped and cleaned they must be dyed the brightest yellow possible. The best dye to use is Venard's yellow which is available from most fly tying supply houses. If Venard dye is unavailable, Rite household dye may be used.

Bright yellow is a difficult color to obtain, especially over the darker quail and dove feathers. Therefore, it will be necessary to use a large amount of dye. When I use Rite dye, I generally use an entire package per dying. Venard's dye is much stronger and usually requires about one-half teaspoon per one-half gallon of water.

The author with a 10 lb. brown taken in western North Carolina.

Chapter One
The "Yallar"
Hammer Series

If you are planning to use your wife's kitchen as your dying area, the next step could save your marriage, not to mention your fly-tying and fishing career. Make certain that you have a large supply of newspapers available and cover the floor and working area thoroughly. This dye, especially Venard's, is extremely difficult to remove if spilled or splattered.

Before starting the dying procedure, make sure that you have all necessary supplies including an old aluminum pot (capable of holding three-fourths to one gallon of water), a wire basket similar to the ones used in deep fat fryers, and a large metal serving spoon. The wire basket should fit inside the aluminum pot without touching the sides. If the basket is too large, it allows the feathers to touch the side of the pot where they can be scorched, rendering them useless.

Fill the aluminum pot with approximately one-half gallon of water, place it on the stove, and bring to a low boil. Once the water begins to boil, add approximately one-fourth cup of vinegar or a couple of tablespoons of salt. This will help to set the dye once the feathers are added. Add the dye and lower the heat to insure that the mixture does not boil over.

Place the feathers in the wire basket (if they have dried out, soak them with cold water). Turn off the heat, immerse the feathers into the dye solution and allow them to soak. It may be necessary to use the spoon to push the feathers into the dye, as they have a tendency to float (the feathers will not take dye properly if allowed to float). The vinegar should set the dye immediately, but I allow them to soak approximately seven to ten minutes to ensure a thorough job.

Once the desired shade has been reached, remove the wire basket and run cold tap water over the feathers, rinsing away all unused dye. It is a good idea to rinse the feathers outside with the garden hose. If you rinse the feathers inside, make certain that you are working over a stainless steel sink, as the dye has a tendency to stain all other materials. Place the feathers on several layers of newspaper and put them in a location where they will dry. When the feathers are dry, you should have a perfect "Yallar" Hammer imitation feather that should be stored in plastic zip lock bags with a few moth balls.

Brook Trout taken by Kevin Howell - 1998

The "Yallar" Hammer Wooly Worm

My research indicates that this is the original "Yallar" Hammer pattern. For many years, it was the only version of the "Yallar" hammer that I saw, though I did see some variations in body color, including white, yellow and black. All versions seem to produce well, but the black one has always been my favorite.

In recent years, I've made one substitution in the fly that I feel has improved its success rate. Instead of using Golden Pheasant for the tail, I've substituted maribou to match the color of the body. Also, at times, I will add four to six strands of Crystal Flash to the tail.

Of the three "Yallar" Hammer patterns discussed here, the Wooly Worm is the easiest to tie and is the most effective.

NOTE: Before tying any "Yallar" Hammer pattern, it will be necessary to fill a container capable of holding six to eight ounces with water. Immerse the prepared feathers into the container of water and allow them to soak until you are ready to use them. Soaking the feathers softens the quill, which makes them flexible. This makes tying a neat fly much easier.

TYING INSTRUCTIONS

Materials needed:

HOOK:	Mustad 9671 - size 8 -14
THREAD:	Black uni-thread
WIRE:	.010 - .020
TAIL:	Golden Pheasant
BODY:	Black floss or wool
HACKLE:	Imitation "Yallar" Hammer feather palmered through body.

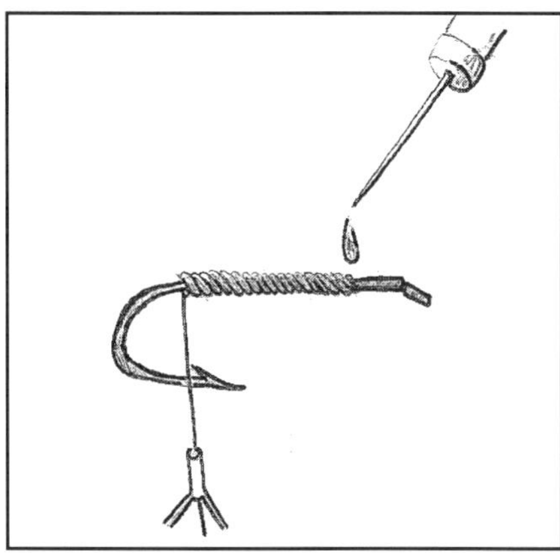

1. Place hook in the vise and wrap hook shank with desired amount of lead. Wrap lead with tying thread and coat with head cement to insure durability.

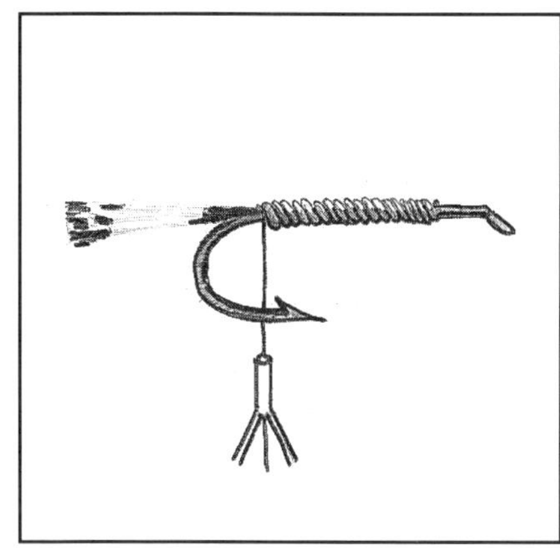

2. Wind thread to bend of hook. Clip 6 to 8 fibers from the tippet feather of a Golden Pheasant. Tie the fibers in as a tail. The length of the tail should be approximately the same as the length of the hook shank.

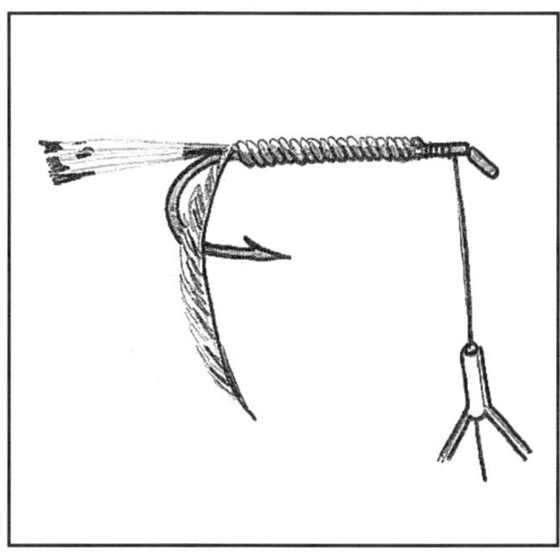

3. Remove a feather that you have been soaking. The feather will have a natural curve to it and the fibers on the inside of the curve are much longer than the fibers on the outside. These long fibers must be removed from the quill before the tying process is started. Take your scissors and clip the long fibers as close to the quill as possible. At the bend of the hook, tie in the small end of the quill with fibers facing you. Some tyers split the quills with a razor blade to prevent building up bulk and to make winding a little easier. I've never found this to be necessary and I only split the quills when tying very small patterns.

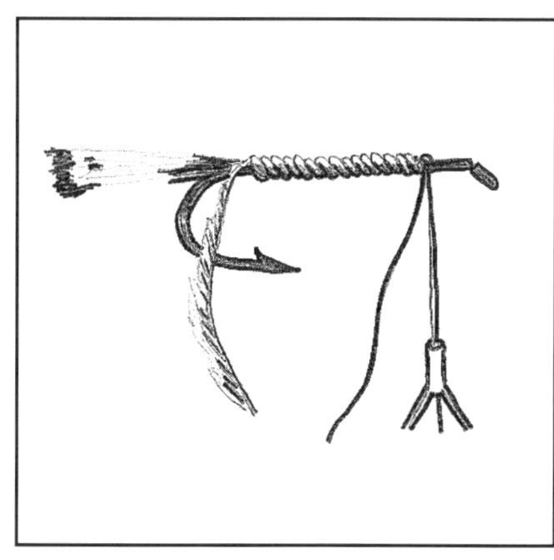

4. Wind the thread to within approximately 1/32 inch of the eye of the hook. Tie in two or three strands of black floss, black wool or black chenille. Floss or chenille should be tied in at bend along with feather.

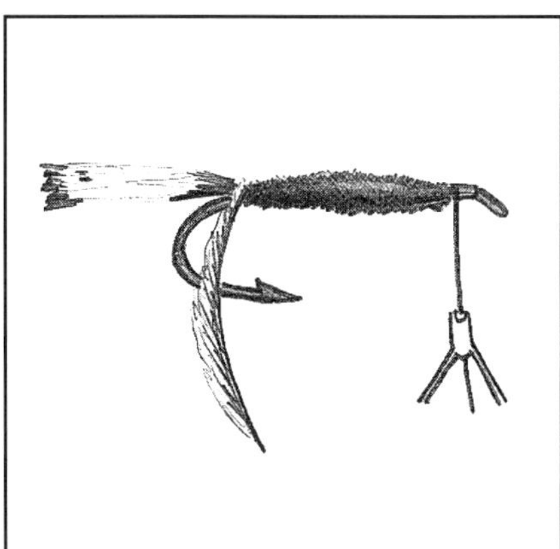

5. Wind the floss back and forth to build a heavy body that is tapered on both ends. After an adequate body is built, tie off and clip the point just behind the eye of the hook.

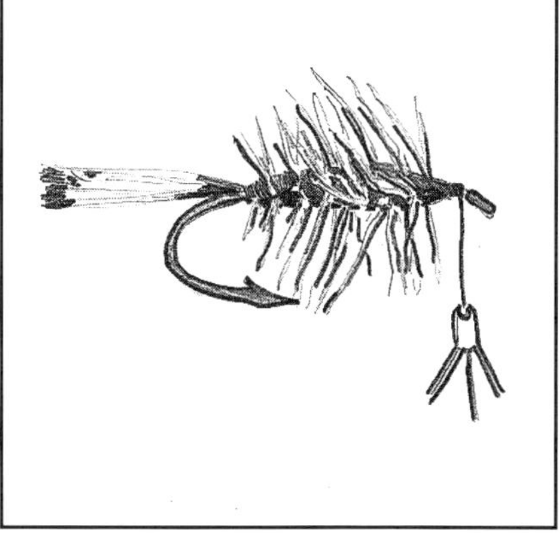

6. Palmer* the "Yallar" Hammer feather to the front of the floss body, allowing black to show between wraps of the feather. Tie off and clip. Build up the head of the fly with your thread. Whip finish and clip the thread.

* The term "palmer" means to wrap the feather from the rear to the front of the body, allowing a small amount of the body material to show between each turn.

7. Remove the fly from the vise. Trim the tips of the "Yallar" Hammer feather. After trimming, the feather should be slightly longer than the gap of the hook. Cement the head.

Chapter One
The "Yallar"
Hammer Series

The "Yallar" Hammer Nymph

TYING INSTRUCTIONS

Materials needed:

HOOK:	Mustad 9671 - size 8 -14
THREAD:	Red uni-thread
LEAD WIRE:	.010 - .020
TAIL:	Soft brown rooster feather barbs
ABDOMEN:	Gold Uni-Floss palmered with Yallar Hammer Feather
WING CASE:	Turkey quill
THORAX:	Yellow wool
HACKLE:	Soft brown rooster saddle or hen hackle

NOTE: Before tying any "Yallar" Hammer pattern, it will be necessary to fill a container capable of holding six to eight ounces with water. Immerse the prepared feathers into the container of water and allow them to soak until you are ready to use them. Soaking the feathers softens the quill, which makes them flexible. This makes tying a neat fly much easier.

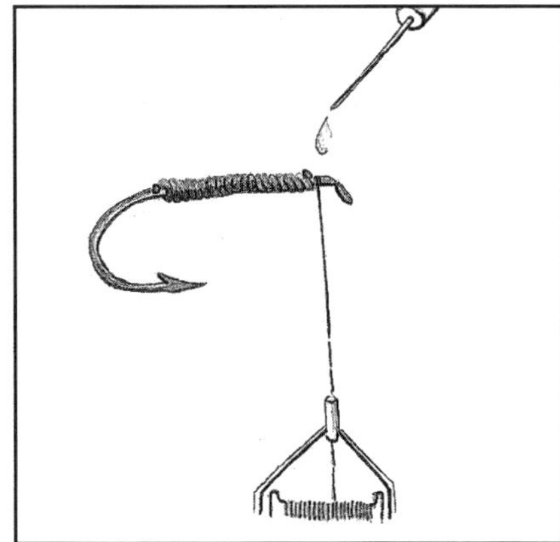

1. Insert the hook into the vise and wrap the shank with desired amount of lead wire. Wrap thread over the lead wire to secure it to the hook. To insure a strong, durable body, coat the lead and thread with fly head cement.

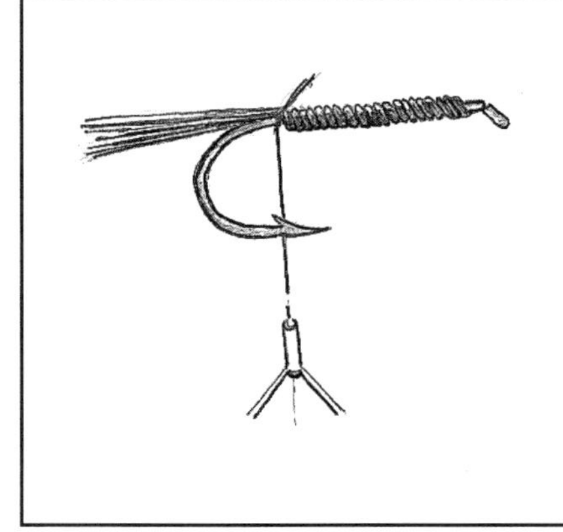

2. Tie in approximately twelve brown rooster fibers for the tail. For proper balance and appearance, the tail should be approximately the same length as the hook shank and angled slightly downward.

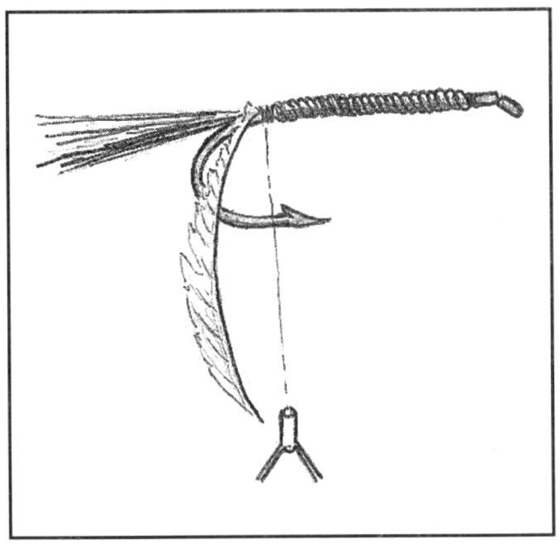

3. Wind the thread back to the bend of the hook. Select an imitation "Yallar" Hammer feather that has been soaking in the water. Use the same procedure for preparing the feather as you used in step 3 for the "Yallar" Hammer Wooly Worm.

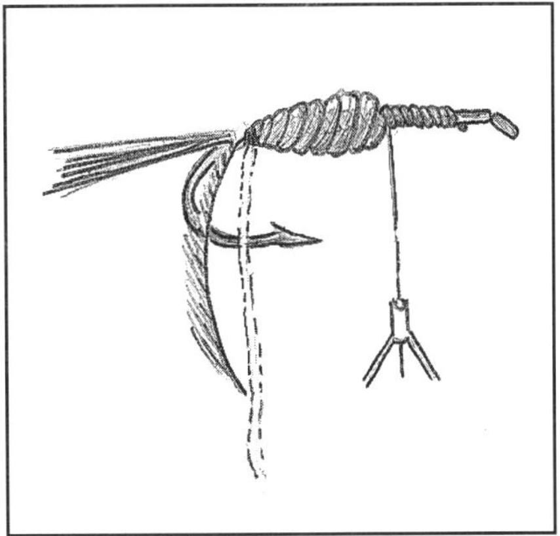

4. Wind the tying thread up the hook's shank until approximately two-thirds of the shank has been covered. At this point, tie in two to four (depending upon the size of the fly) strands of gold floss and form a tapered body.

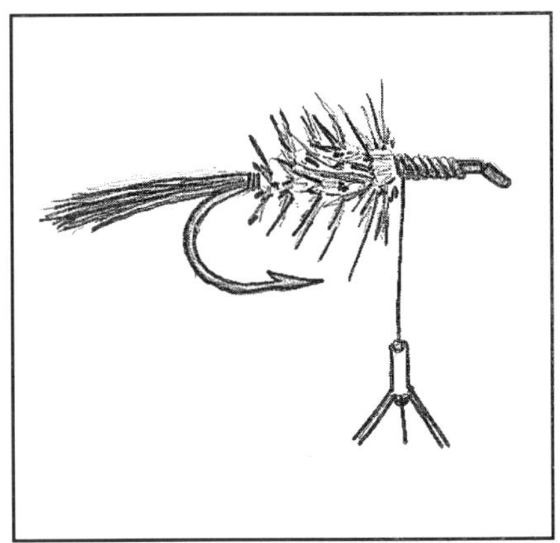

5. Palmer* the quill over the tapered body allowing a slight amount of the gold floss to show between each wrap. Tie off the quill. Remove the fly from the vise and clip the fibers. Clip the fibers with the same taper as the floss body you formed. After clipping, the fibers should be approximately 1/32 inch in length.

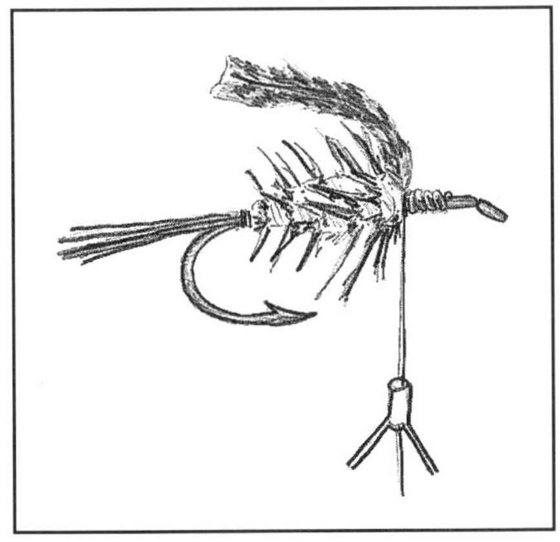

6. Re-insert the fly into the vise and tie in a small strip of turkey quill on top of the hook. Make sure the quill lays back over the fly's body. (Be sure to spray the quill with clear Krylon before tying onto the hook. This will increase the durability of your fly.)

7. Tie in medium size, bright yellow wool at the same point as the turkey quill. Build a thorax and trim off excess. (A couple of substitutions can be made at this point. You can substitute medium chenille for the wool or you can use your dubbing needle to pick out some of the wool fibers to give the fly a more buggy appearance.)

8. Tie in a soft, brown rooster hackle in front of the wool. Make approximately four to six turns of the hackle, tie off and clip excess. With your fingers, pull the hackle fibers back over and under the body and wrap over the hackles three or four times to insure that the fibers point toward the rear of the hook. This procedure is called the "collar" method. As you wrap over the hackle, be sure to let up on thread tension or the collar will flare.

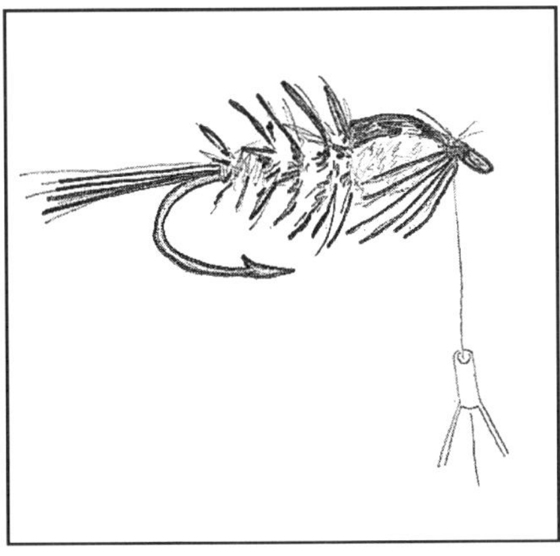

9. Clip the hackle off of the top of the fly. Pull the turkey quill over the top of the thorax, tie off and clip excess. Build thread head. Whip finish. Cement thread. Cement the fly and you now have a perfect "Yallar" Hammer Nymph.

* The term "palmer" means to wrap the feather from the rear to the front of the body, allowing a small amount of the body material to show between each turn.

The "Yallar" Hammer Dry Fly

TYING INSTRUCTIONS

NOTE: Before tying any "Yallar" Hammer pattern, it will be necessary to fill a container capable of holding 6 to 8 ounces with water. Immerse the prepared feathers into the container of water and allow them to soak until you are ready to use them. Soaking the feathers softens the quill, which makes them flexible. This makes tying a neat fly much easier.

Materials needed:

HOOK:	Mustad 94840 - size 10 -16
TAIL:	Light ginger hackle fibers
BODY:	Gold floss palmered with imitation Yallar Hammar quill
WINGS:	Barred wood duck flank
HACKLE:	Light ginger

Cascade on the beautiful South Mills River in western North Carolina. Photo by Kevin Howell.

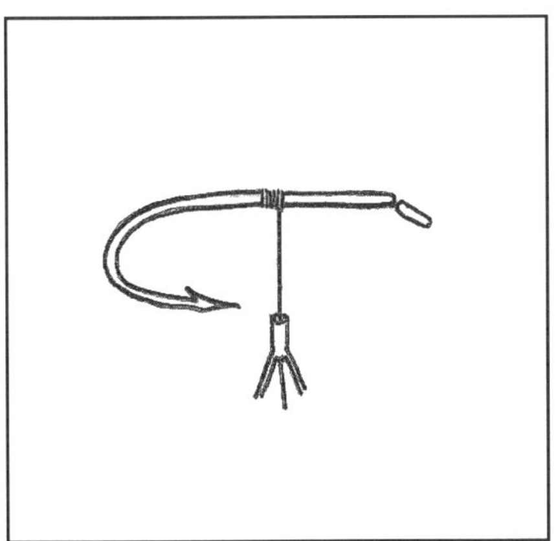

1. Insert the hook into the vise and attach thread in the middle of the hook shank.

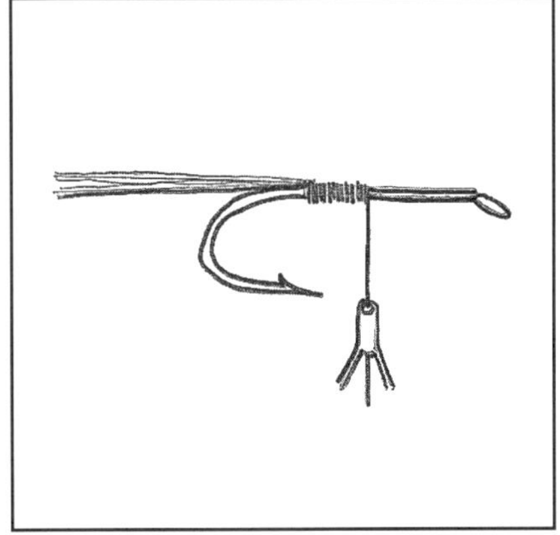

2. Select a large, high quality ginger hackle feather free of web. Gently pull your index finger and thumb down the hackle to even the tips of the fibers. Pull a group of fibers from the quill and tie them in for a tail. For proper balance and appearance, the tail should be one and one-half times the length of the hook shank. At this point, the tail should stick straight out the rear of the hook and should not point up or down.

Chapter One
The "Yallar" Hammer Series

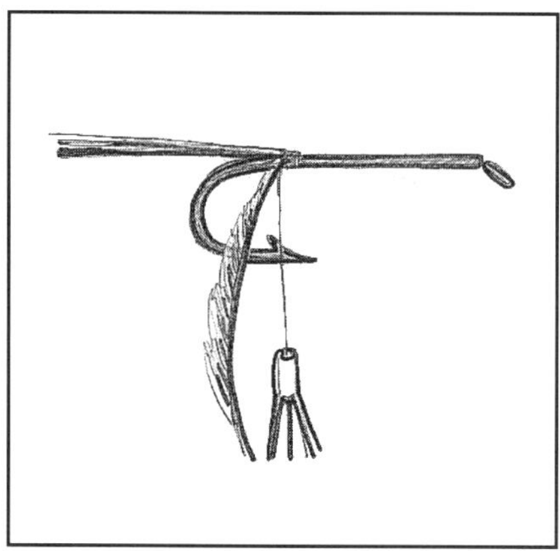

3. Wind the thread to the bend of the hook. Select a small quill that has been soaking in water. Trim all the fibers from the large side of the quill. (see step 3 for tying "yallar" hammer nymph) Tie the small end of the quill onto the hook, making sure the remaining fibers on the quill are facing you.

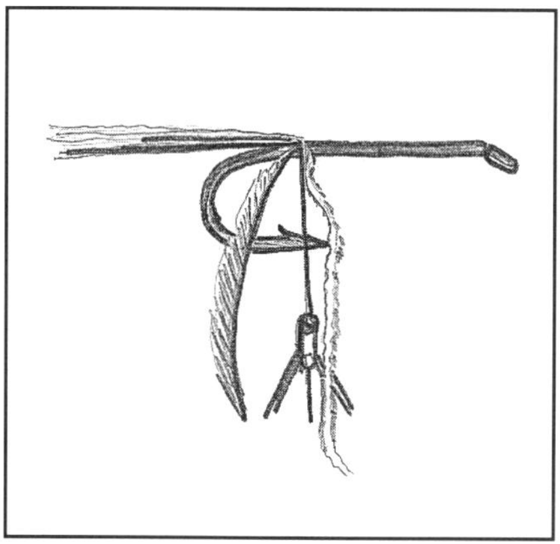

4. At the same point you tied in the quill, tie in two to four strands (depending on size of fly being tied) of gold floss. Clip off excess.

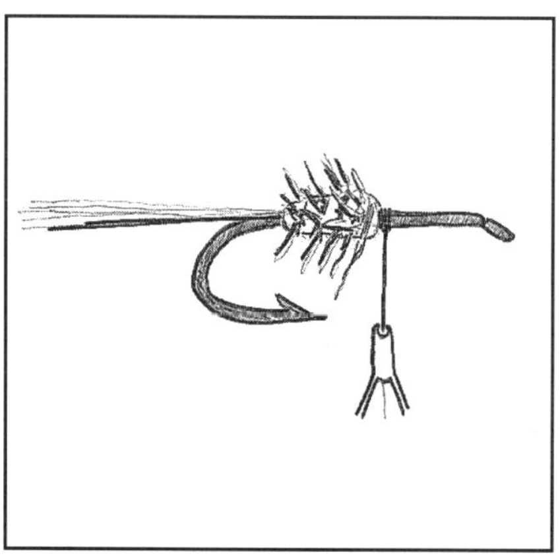

5. Wind the thread toward the eye of the hook, stopping approximately 1/3 length of the hook shank from the eye. Tie in and form a tapered body with the gold floss. Clip off excess floss and palmer the "yallar" hammer quill over the tapered body, allowing a slight amount of the gold floss to show between each wrap. Tie off the quill and clip excess. Remove the fly from the vise and clip the fibers that are sticking out from the body. Clip the quill following the taper of the body, leaving only a small amount sticking out from the body.

Kevin Howell on western North Carolina's Whitewater River. Photo by John Brinkley.

Chapter One
The "Yallar"
Hammer Series

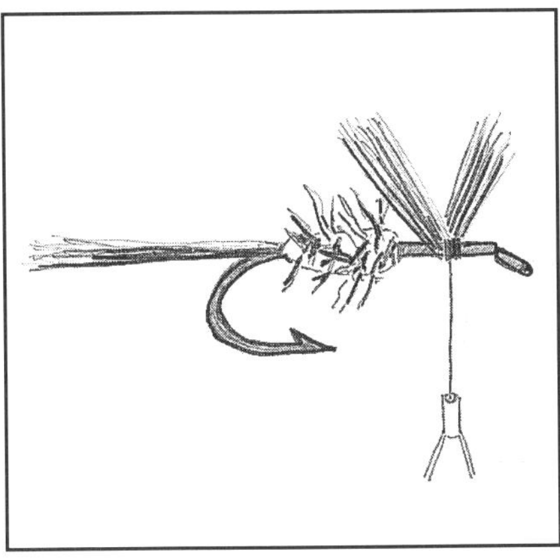

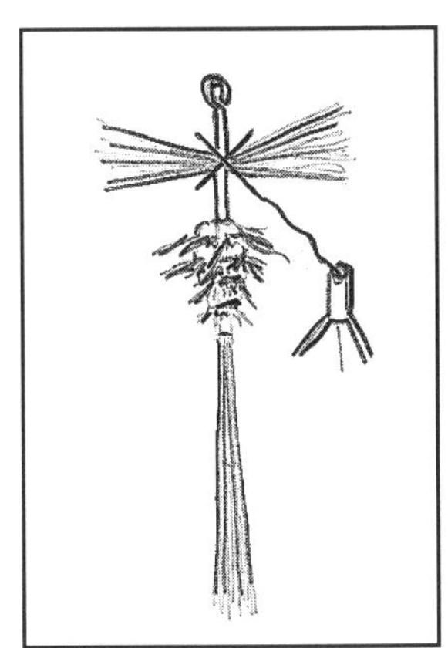

6. Insert fly back into the vise. Select a lemon colored barred wood duck flank feather to use as wings. On each side of the wood duck quill, cut matching portions of the fibers. In front of the body you just formed, lay the fibers on top of the hook with the tips extending over the eye of the hook. At this point, the thread should be positioned in the middle of the empty space in front of the body. Wind the thread over the fibers several times to secure them to the hook. With the index finger and thumb on your left hand, pull the fiber back until it forms a ninety-degree angle with the hook. Wind the thread in front of the fibers several times. When the feathers are released, they should remain in the ninety-degree position. Take the point of the scissors or bodkin and divide the feathers into equal parts. Using the figure-eight method, wind your thread between the two clumps of feathers. You should now have a perfect set of divided wings.

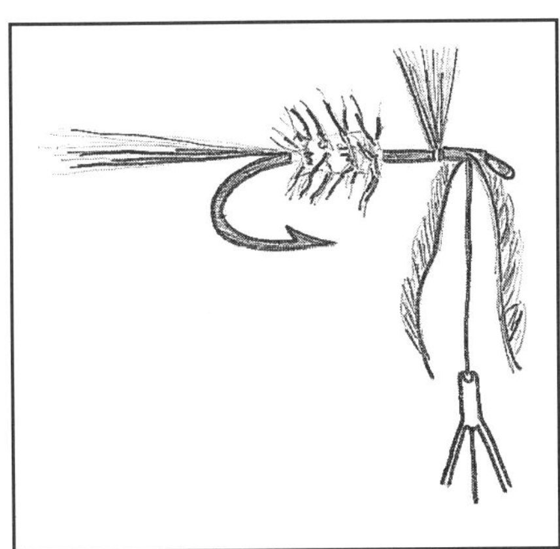

7. Wind your thread back to the front of your body. Select two light ginger hackles that are suitable for the size hook you are using. (When you select a proper hackle, its width should be one and one-half times the gap of the hook.) At the butt of the hackles, clip all of the "webby" fibers as close to the stem of the hackle as possible. In front of the body, tie in the two hackles you clipped. Wind thread to the eye of the hook. With your hackle pliers, wind the hackle behind and in front of the wings. To ensure a pleasing appearance and proper balance, you should make equal number of turns of the hackle behind and in front of the wings. Whip finish and cement the fly.

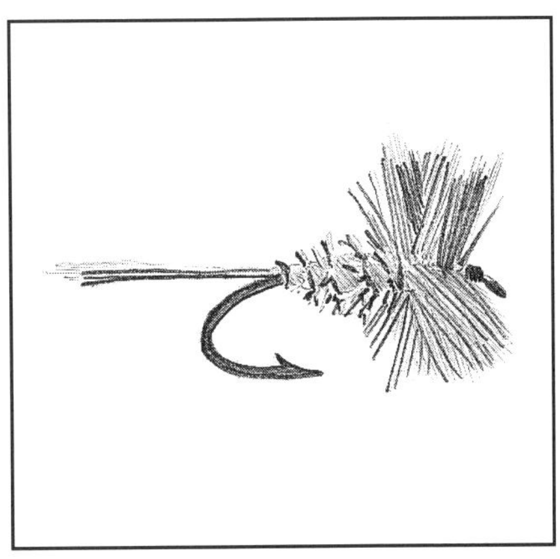

The "Yallar" Hammer Dry Fly

Chapter Two

The Sheep Fly

As I slowly parted the laurel and peeked into the pool, I was pleasantly shocked at the sight of two large brown trout slowly swimming in a circle. They were approximately twenty-four and twenty-six inches in length.

Gently, I eased away from the pool and reentered the stream approximately fifty yards below. I worked carefully into position at the bottom of the pool and allowed the trout to circle a couple of times to make sure they were not alarmed. It seemed to take a lifetime, but I waited until the two trout began to make the turn on their third trip in front of me, then made my cast. The fly dropped fourteen inches in front of the lead trout. Neither fish reacted to the cast, as they continued on their path. As the lead trout reached the fly, she simply opened her mouth and sucked it in. Moments later, I slid the net under a twenty-six inch beauty that weighed slightly more than six pounds. This was my introduction to fishing the Sheep Fly for large trout.

A review of my fishing diary indicates that the first summer that my brother, Dwight, and I used the Sheep Fly, we caught and released thirty-two trout over eighteen inches in the public streams of North Carolina. In July of 1991, I was fortunate enough to take a thirty inch brown (the largest of my career) that weighed ten pounds on a size eight Sheep Fly. Therefore, you can understand why I consider the Sheep Fly the Cadillac of all nymphs. If I had to be limited to one pattern to fish with for the remainder of my fishing days, it would be the Sheep Fly.

As far as appearance is concerned, the Sheep Fly could be considered the ugly duckling of all flies. If they didn't know the fly's reputation, most fishermen would pass over it when selecting a fly. Dwight and I were showing the fly and describing our success with it to a famous fly fisherman and fly shop owner in Montana. He laughed, saying that he couldn't give the fly away, much less sell it.

Although we call the fly a nymph, it's really not. It appears to be a hybrid between a wet fly, streamer, and nymph, and I'm not really convinced that it gives the appearance of an insect to the trout. The long, variegated wings that lay over the fly's body could give the impression of being a small minnow. We've caught all species on this fly, ranging from carp to largemouth bass. It works especially well on the cannibalistic species.

Chapter Two
The Sheep Fly

In this area, many fishermen refer to the fly as the Howell Fly because they think that Dwight and I developed the pattern. We didn't, and I'm not sure that it would have been included in this book if we had. We may have kept it as our secret, pet, lunker fly.

The Sheep Fly was given to us by the late George "Cap" Weise. Cap was from Lenior, NC , and was headmaster of the Patterson School for Boys. For many years Cap was basically a dry fly purist. This quickly changed when Cap started fishing the Sheep Fly, as he soon became a Sheep Fly purist.

The Sheep Fly was developed by one of Cap's friends, Newland Sanders, from Lenior, and it soon developed a group of followers in that area. Although the fly was developed and fished almost exclusively in North Carolina, its reputation is spreading to other areas. We have used the fly in New York, Montana, Wyoming, Idaho, and Canada. It works as well in those areas as in the Southern Appalachians.

Wilson Creek, western North Carolina. Note the thick streamside vegetation typical of Southern Appalachian trout streams. Photo by Kevin Howell.

Chapter Two
The Sheep Fly

The Sheep Fly

TYING INSTRUCTIONS

Materials needed:

HOOK:	Mustad 9671 or 79580
THREAD:	Black uni-thread
TAIL:	Soft brown rooster or hen hackle.
BODY:	Muskrat back with guard hairs left in
HACKLE:	Soft brown rooster or hen hackle
WINGS:	Dark cast grizzly hackle tips
WIRE:	.015 to .030

Don Ray and Dwight Howell display the results of their angling skill at an early age. Don Ray, age four, and Dwight, age ten, on the New River in Todd, North Carolina.

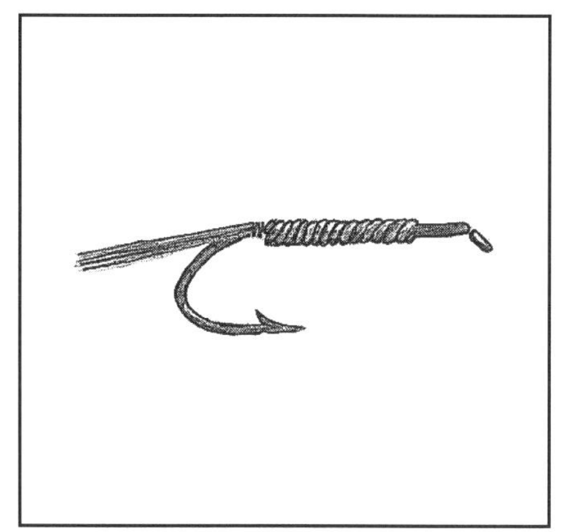

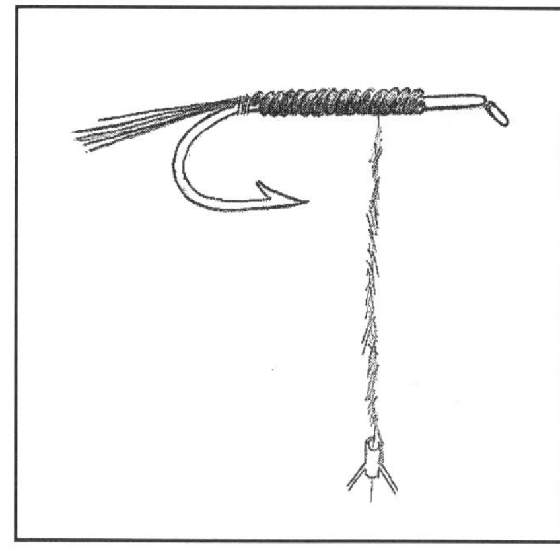

1. Insert the hook in the vise and wrap with desired amount of lead wire. Wrap lead with thread and coat with head cement.

2. Wind thread to the bend of the hook to form a tail of approximately twelve to fourteen brown hackle fibers. For appearance and balance, the tail should be the same length as the shank of the hook.

3. Wind thread to the base of the tail and wax the thread thoroughly with a good quality tacky dubbing wax. To improve durability, some tiers use rubber cement as dubbing wax. Trim the fur from the back of a muskrat pelt. Be sure to leave guard hairs in the fur. Place the fur in a blender and blend the fur and guard hairs together. Spin the blended fur onto the waxed thread. (If you prefer, you can form a loop and spin the dubbing between the threads of the loop.)

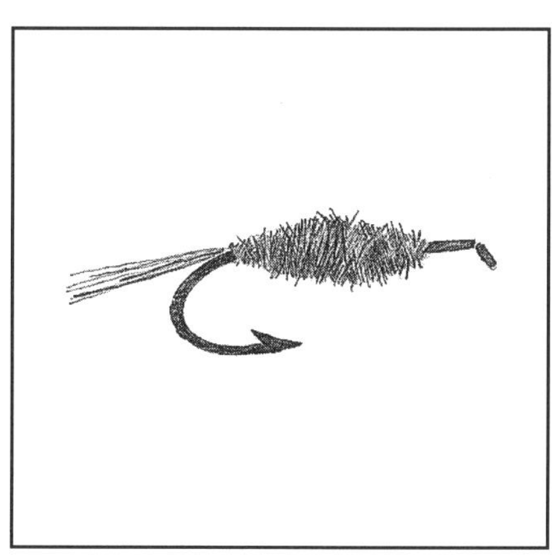

4. Build an oversized body with the dubbing material. Body must be tapered on both ends. In order for the wings to lay on the fly properly, the body most be tapered in the front as well as the rear. After forming the body, use your dubbing needle to pick the body, creating a fuzzy appearance (the fuzzier the better).

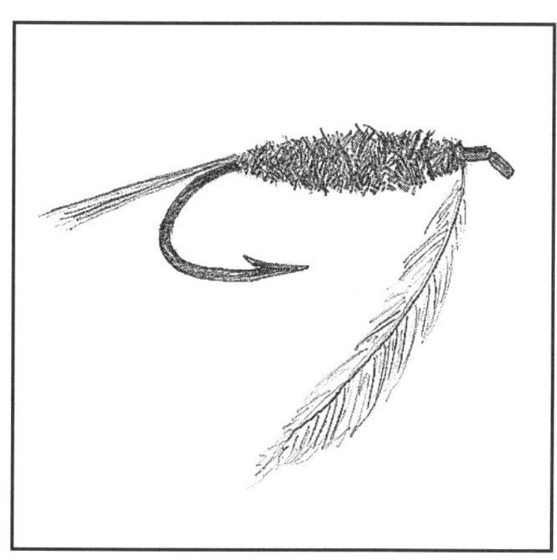

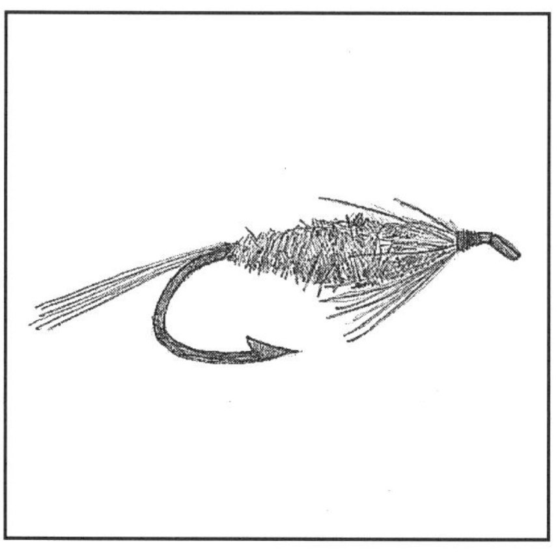

5. Tie in a slightly oversized (about one size larger than normal) brown hackle in front of the body. Make approximately six turns of the hackle, tie off and clip excess. With your fingers, pull all hackle fibers back over and under the body. Wrap over the base of the hackle with the tying thread. When the hackle fibers are released, they should continue to lay over the fly's body, collar style.

6. Select two small grizzly hackles to be used as wings. Once the hackles have been pulled from the cape, you will notice that they have a natural curve. Place the curves back to back and lay them on top of the fly, making sure they extend to the rear of the body. Tie the wings off, clip excess and build a neat head with the thread. Cement and allow to dry.

Note: When the wings are tied in properly, they should lay almost flat on the back of the fly. If they stand up, it's an indication that the front of the body does not have enough taper.

Chapter Three

The Hot Creek Special

As a young boy, my son, Kevin, always enjoyed spending time in my fly shop imitating me. To pacify him and to keep him occupied, I set up one of my discarded vises and gave him a set of tying tools. He would often take my trimmings, wrap them around a hook, and sell his special flies to his Papa (grandfather).

One day while I was tying Zug Bugs, Kevin kept pestering me for materials. I gave him some peacock herl that I trimmed from the Zug Bugs. He took the trimmings and wrapped them on his hook. When he handed me his crude creation, it surprised me how much it resembled a bug. It dawned on me that peacock is used in most of the best-producing flies, its iridescent sheen attracting trout under all conditions.

When the pattern was developed, it was late July, and oppressively hot. It had not rained in several days. "Dog Days Trout" are difficult to catch, but extremely clear water and bright sunlight makes them even more of a challenge. My favorite late summer fishing spot at the time was South Toe River (Yancey County, NC), an extremely clear, free-stone stream. On our weekly trip to the South Toe, my brother, father, and I would always bet a dollar on the largest trout. I made two dollars a week for several weeks before I revealed the secret fly I was using. Since the fly had been so productive in low, clear water, I deemed it the Hot Creek Special.

This fly is lightly weighted with a small amount of .010 or .015 lead wire which causes it to sink only slightly below the surface film. Since it is so lightly weighted, it hits the water with a very soft "kerplunk", which imitates a terrestrial dropping into the water.

When fishing this pattern, I use a long leader, usually eleven feet, with a longer than usual tippet. I grease the leader with fly line dressing all the way to, and including, one-half of the tippet. This helps the leader to float. After making my cast, I watch the tippet where it enters the water for the telltale twitch or hesitation. Although this fly has not produced the number of really large trout that other flies described in this book have, it continues to be my number one fly for late summer and fall fishing.

TYING INSTRUCTIONS

Materials needed:

HOOK:	Mustad 3399 size 10 - 14
TAIL:	Olive hackle fibers
BODY:	Peacock herl
LEGS:	Peacock herl
BACK:	Turkey quill

1. Insert hook in vise and wrap wire on the shank of the hook. Wrap thread over the lead wire to secure it to the hook. To insure a strong durable body, coat the lead with fly cement.

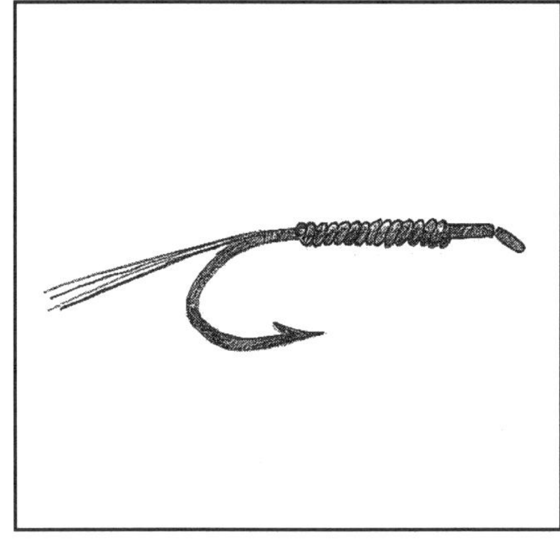

2. Wind thread to the bend of the hook and tie in eight-to-twelve olive hackle fibers. Length of tail should be approximately the same length as the shank of the hook. After being tied in, the tail should point downward slightly.

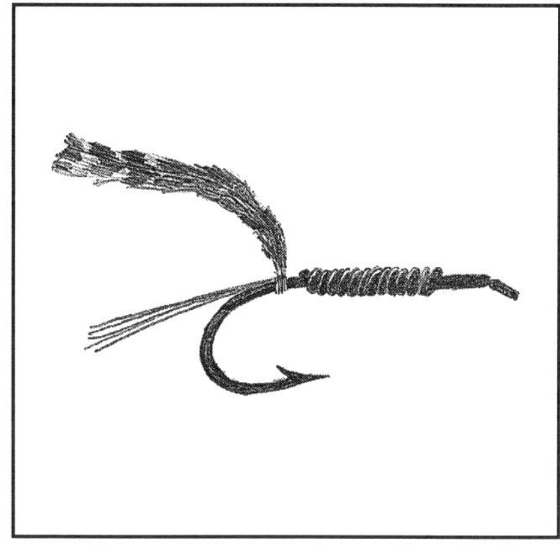

3. At the base of the tail, tie in a strip of turkey quill. For durability, the quill should be sprayed with clear Krylon before it is tied onto the hook.

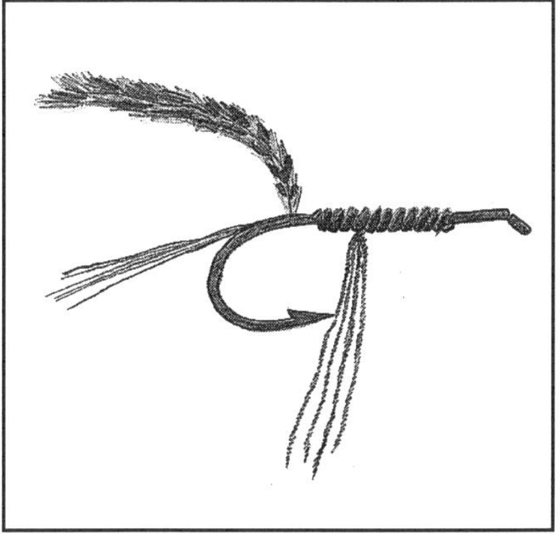

4. Tie in three strands of peacock herl at the same point that the turkey quill was tied in.

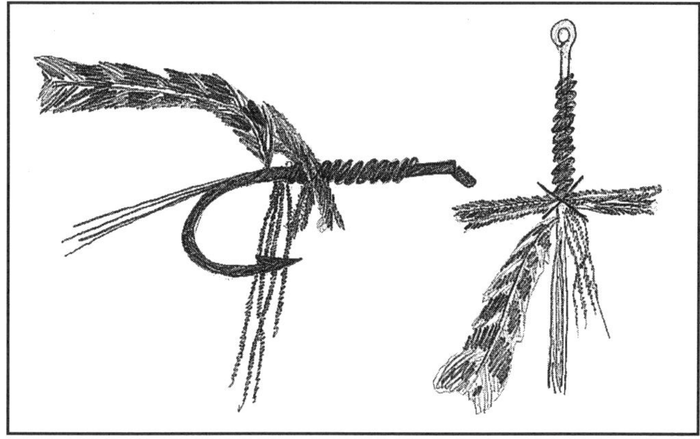

5. Wind your thread one-third of the way up the hook shank. At this point lay two peacock herls across the top of the hook, making sure the hook is at the centering point of the herl. Using the figure-eight method, tie the herl to the hook.

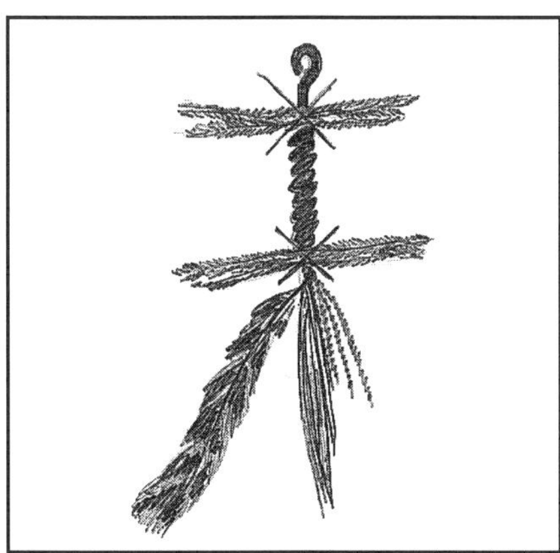

6. Wind thread forward covering another one-third of the hook. At this point in the tying procedure, two-thirds of the hook should be covered with thread and one-third should be barren. Select two more peacock herls and tie them onto the hook the same as you did in step five.

7. Wind thread forward to the eye of the hook. Coat entire hook shank with fly cement. Wind peacock herl forward to eye of the hook. If necessary, wind peacock herl back and forth across the hook shank to build up the desired body thickness. Tie off herl at eye of hook and clip the excess. Clip peacock herl you tied in for legs.

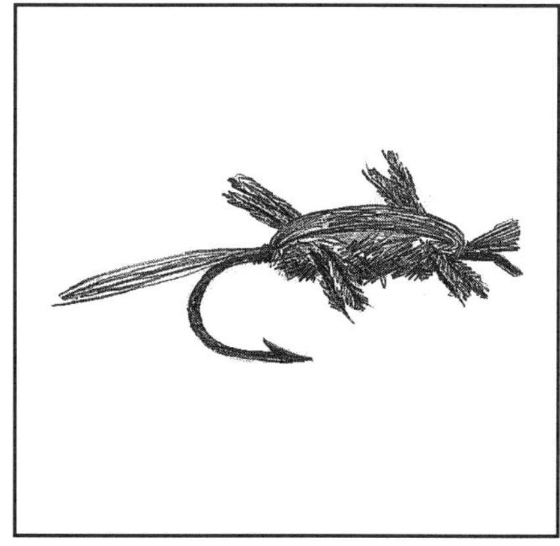

8. Pull turkey quill over the back of the fly and tie off at the eye. Clip the excess allowing a small amount to stick out beyond where it was tied off. Whip finish and cement.

Chapter Four

Bill's Provider

This fly was designed and given to me by my good friend and fishing companion Bill Hale, from Anderson, SC. When I asked Bill why he developed the fly, his reply was, "Rubber legs". One of Bill's favorite nymphs is the Bitch Creek, which features large, white rubber legs. However, he realized that the productivity of the fly diminishes when the water is extremely clear, because of its white legs. Therefore, he wanted to develop a new nymph that featured many of the characteristics of the Bitch Creek, but would produce in ultra-clear water conditions.

In thinking about fly designs, Bill realized the fish-catching ability of the wooly worm, peacock herl, and rubber leg. He then combined these three qualities to create his new pattern. When he gave me the sample, he remarked that it would always provide some fish. Therefore, it became known as Bill's Provider.

In my opinion, the fish-catching ability of any nymph can be increased one hundred percent by the addition of rubber legs. As the fly drifts downstream, the legs wiggle as it encounters different currents. A trout following the fly, undecided about striking, is often convinced or suckered into believing the fly is alive or is about to get away when the legs start moving. Most trout will not allow an easy, uninjured meal to escape, and strike without hesitation.

The first opportunity I had to fish the fly was on the lower Gallatin River just outside of Bozeman, Montana. At the time I was enjoying an extended fishing vacation with my father and oldest son, Kevin.

We had heard rumors of a local fisherman catching some extremely large browns, including one that weighed slightly more than twelve pounds out of the Gallatin. These fish were being caught on live bullheads or sculpins. These rumors were enough to convince us to spend a couple of days frothing the waters of the Gallatin.

Kevin, much younger at the time, was not yet the confirmed, diehard fly fishing purist he is today. Since his major goal was to catch an extremely large trout, the tales of big trout taken on live scuplins were more than he could endure. He opted to use bullheads on our first outing on the Gallatin. I was eager to try Bill's new fly. Therefore, I selected the Provider.

Chapter Four
Bill's Provider

The Provider outfished the bullheads about three-to-one. As a matter of fact, the Provider was so productive that I could often catch a fish in a run that Kevin had just fished with bullheads. Bullheads are the preferred food of western trout, and very seldom can they be outfished with flies - but the Provider did it.

Incidently, we started tying the Provider commercially, and it is one of our top selling nymphs along with the "Yallar" Hammer, Kevin's Stone, and the Sheep Fly. Evidently, our customers must feel that it is as productive in eastern streams as we found it to be in Montana.

Where every productive fishing trip begins. Don Ray and Kevin Howell hard at work in the fly shop. Photo courtesy of the Transylvania Times.

Bill's Provider

TYING INSTRUCTIONS

Materials needed:

HOOK:	Mustad 9671 size 10 - 6
REAR LEGS:	Brown rubber legs size medium
BODY:	Peacock herl
HACKLE:	Brown - palmered over peacock body
FRONT LEGS:	same as back legs
THREAD:	6/0 Eagle river - chartreuse

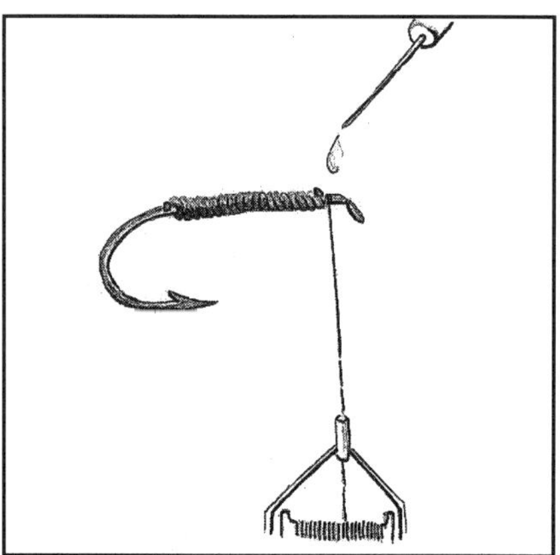

1. Insert hook in vise and wrap shank with desired amount of lead wire. Wrap thread over lead wire to secure it to the hook. To insure a strong, durable body, coat the lead and thread with fly head cement.

2. Cut two sections, approximately one and one-half inches in length, from a single strand of brown rubber leg material. Fold one section into two equal parts and place center of the fold on top of the hook behind the lead wire. Secure legs in position with your thread. If legs are too close together, spread and use a figure-eight wrap with the thread to hold legs in correct position.

Chapter Four
Bill's Provider

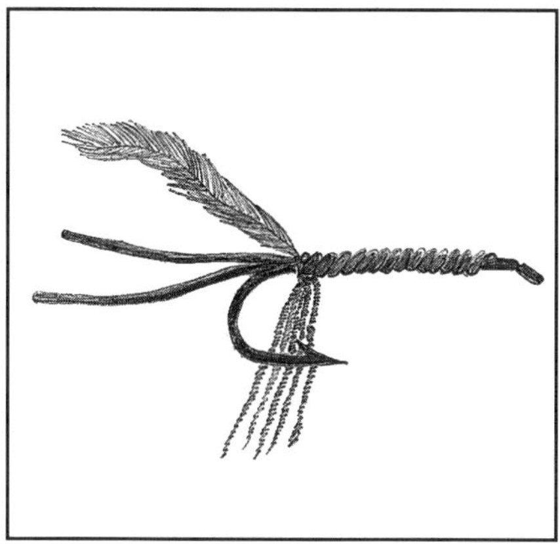

3. Tie in a soft, brown hackle and 5 to 8 (depending on body size desired) strands of peacock herl in the same position as the rubber leg.

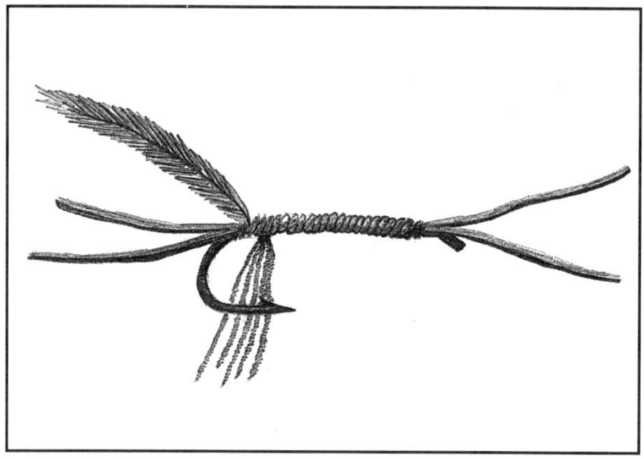

4. Wind thread to eye of hook and attach the front rubber legs in same fashion as described in step one.

5. Wind peacock herl back and forth between bend of hook and eye, building desired thickness of body. Tie off peacock herl at eye of hook. Wind thread back and forth through the body to improve durability. At this point, the thread should be at the eye of the hook.

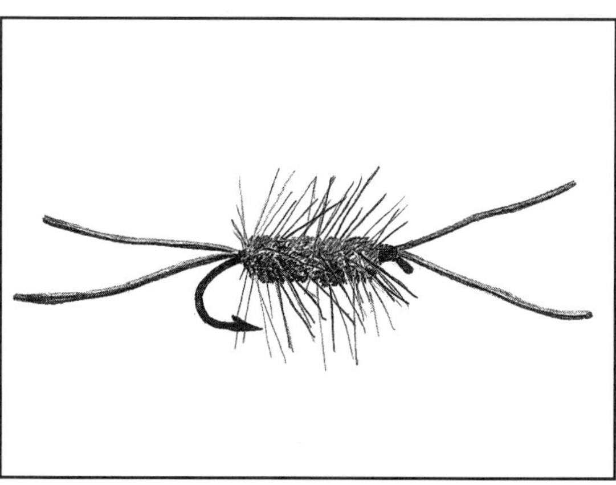

6. Palmer the hackle over the body allowing a slight amount of the herl to show between each turn of the hackle.

7. Tie off hackle at eye. Build up head, clip thread and cement.

Chapter Five

The Bug

If you have a nymph that contains a fuzzy body, flash, sparkle, a peacock body or rubber legs, you probably have a successful, fish producing nymph. If you have a nymph that meets all of these criteria, you have the "Mother" of all flies.

"The Bug" that I developed in 1990 meets all of these criteria, though I wasn't overly impressed with it at that time. For this reason, I placed it in my fly box, forgot about it, and continued to use my old standby patterns.

One day late in August, I was fishing one of my favorite streams. The weather was oppressively hot and the stream extremely low. I wasn't catching much, though I'd tried all my low water flies and techniques. Out of desperation, I opened my fly box, searching for a fly to try when my eyes fell upon "The Bug". On my first cast, after attaching "The Bug" to my line, I took a fourteen inch brownie. My first thought was that I had finally found a crazy trout that wanted to feed. Three casts later, I took another nice brown. Shortly afterwards, I was releasing a heavy bodied twenty-one incher. This continued all afternoon. When dark fell, I ended one of the best days fishing that I'd had in several years.

It is possible that the trout started striking about the time I switched to "The Bug". I should have changed to some other pattern to see if the trout would continue to strike, but I was having too much fun. Regardless of the reason the fish were striking, I built a great deal of confidence in this fly, and it has been a constant producer of nice trout ever since.

Chapter Five
The Bug

TYING INSTRUCTIONS

Materials needed:

HOOK:	Mustad 9671 size 8 - 14
TAIL:	Grey rubber - size medium
BODY:	Peacock palmered with grizzly and brown hackle
RIB:	Gold bead wire
REAR LEGS:	Grey rubber - size medium
FRONT LEGS:	same as back legs
THREAD:	Uni-thread grey

1. Insert the hook into the vise and wrap the shank with the desired amount of lead wire. Wrap thread over the lead wire to secure it to the hook. To insure a strong, durable body, coat the lead and thread with fly head cement.

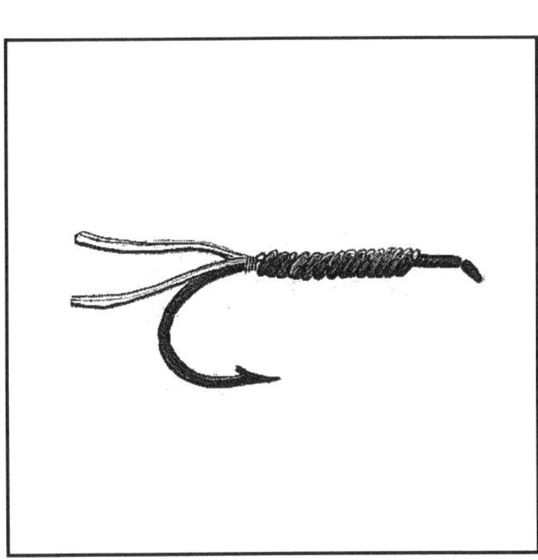

2. Cut a section, approximately 1-1/2 inches in length from a single strand of small grey rubber leg material. Fold into two equal sections and place center of the fold on top of the hook behind the lead wire. Secure legs in position with your thread. If legs are too close together, spread and use a figure-eight wrap with the thread to hold in correct position.

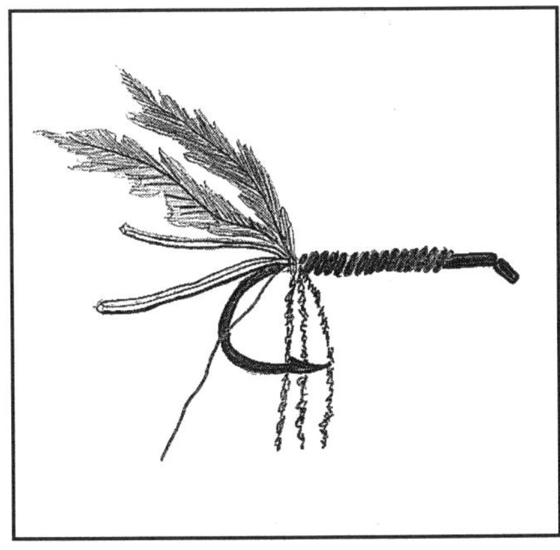

3. Tie in a soft brown and a soft grizzly hackle in the same position as the rubber legs. Also, at this same point, tie in four or five strands of peacock herl and the gold wire that will be used to rib the fly.

Chapter Five
The Bug

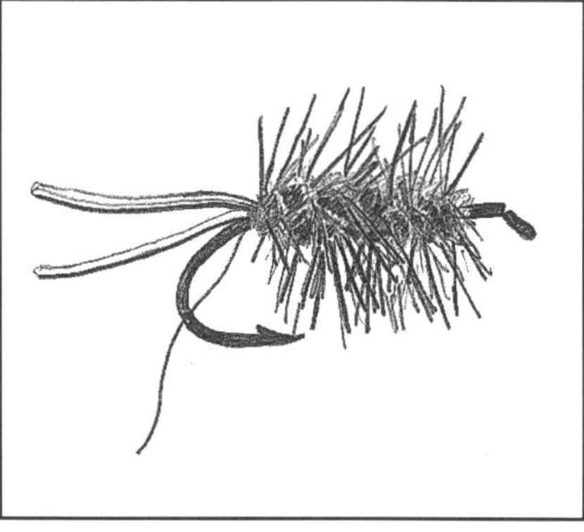

4. Wind peacock herl back and forth between bend of hook and eye. (Be sure to leave enough space at eye to form a head when tying off the fly.) Tie off peacock herl at eye of hook. Wind thread back and forth through the body to improve durability. At this point, the thread should be at the eye of the hook.

5. Palmer the brown and grizzly hackle over the peacock body. Tie off and clip excess.

Don Howell on the Madison River in Montana, 1996.

Chapter Five
The Bug

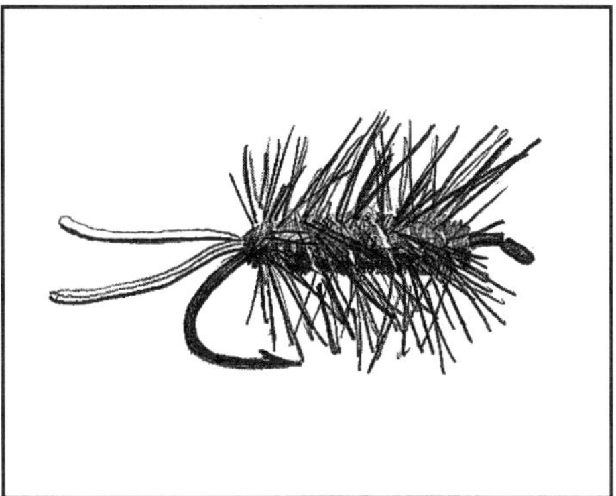

6. Wind gold wire over hackles that were palmered. Tie off and clip excess.

7. Remove fly from the vise. Trim the hackles until they are approximately the same length as the gap of the hook. (Note: On each side of the hook, just behind the eye, trim the hackles close to the body. This will allow the front rubber legs to lay closer to the body.)

8. Re-insert the fly into the vise. Select two strands of grey leg material that are stuck together (do not separate). Cut the legs into a 1-1/2 inch section. Fold the legs in the middle. Place the legs on top of the hook just behind the eye. Using the figure-eight method, secure the legs to the hook. After tying the legs onto the hook, they should form a ninety-degree angle with each side of the hook.

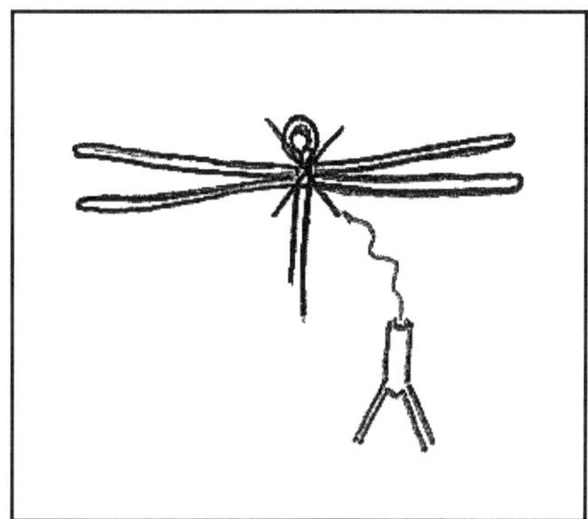

8b. With the left index finger and thumb, pull the legs back along the sides of the body. Wrap over the legs with thread to form a head and secure the legs in position. Use caution, as tight thread tension will cause legs to flare. Clip off thread.

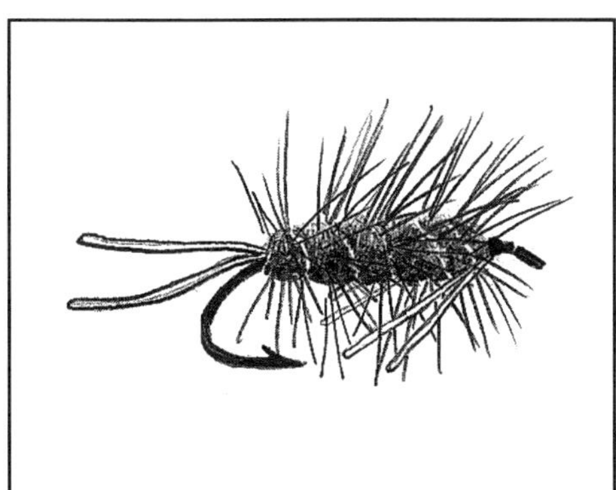

9. Stretch the legs on one side and cut through the leg material slowly. This will cause the legs to separate and pop into proper position of the fly. Repeat the process on the other side of the fly. Remove from vise and cement. (Note: When cementing the fly, do not drop cement on the legs. This will cause them to curl, destroying the shape of the fly.)

Chapter Six

Superfly

Realistic fly patterns have never turned me on very much. They are extremely difficult and time consuming to tie. Usually they are constructed from hard, synthetic materials, and although they look realistic to the fisherman, I feel they must not appear realistic to the trout because they are usually not good trout producers. It has been my experience that when trout are fooled by realistic imitations, they strike the fly, but will not hold onto it because of the unnatural feel of the materials used in its construction.

With this in mind, I wasn't very impressed when Renaud Pelliter, my fly tying and fishing buddy, came by my house to show me a realistic stonefly nymph that he had tied. I couldn't believe my eyes when he revealed the fly to me. It was so realistic, it would have been difficult to distinguish the imitation from a natural. The fly was created from soft, natural materials used in the construction of effective fly patterns.

Renaud told me that he had found tying instructions for the fly in *Sports Afield* magazine. The fly's back and abdomen were constructed from different shades of turkey quills, the legs were tied from brown goose biots, and the thorax was dubbed and picked rabbit fur.

I was intrigued with this fly's construction and appearance, and felt compelled to tie and try a few. Much to my surprise, this realistic fly was extremely productive. Renaud and I not only caught lots of trout using this fly, but some really big ones.

Although the materials used in the fly's construction were extremely realistic, they were not very durable, and the quality turkey quills needed to tie the fly were very expensive and difficult to obtain. Therefore, Renaud and I decided to experiment with materials in the hopes of finding a more durable and accessible material, while retaining the realistic illusion. After several attempts, we decided to use swannundaze for the fly's body. We were extremely worried about substituting the hard swannundaze for the soft turkey quill body, and felt it would probably reduce the effectiveness of the fly. After fishing the new version, however, we found them just as productive, and much more durable than the original. Needless to say, my opinion of realistic patterns has changed.

My best results with this nymph have been in the deepest, darkest, swiftest runs in the river. There are probably two reasons for this success. First of all, the superfly is heavily weighted, which allows it to reach the bottom quickly. Also, most stoneflies live in this type of water. Browns and rainbows wait in these runs for a juicy stonefly to become dislodged and swept to them.

Chapter Six
Superfly

When fishing this nymph, I use a short leader usually seven and one-half feet, and no longer than nine feet. The fly is weighted extremely heavy, and the shorter leader makes casting easier, allowing the nymph to sink quicker and ride closer to the bottom. Monofilament leaders float, and a long leader has a tendency to lift the fly toward the surface. This is one nymph that definitely needs to be fished close to the bottom.

One of my most memorable fishing trips came about as result of this fly. My brother, Dwight, two of our friends, and I had flown to Montana to enjoy some Blue Ribbon trout fishing. The first week we traveled throughout Livingston, Enis and the Dillon area catching trout and putting one thousand miles on a rental car. At the end of the first week, our friends had to return to North Carolina. Dwight and I stayed another week, and rented a cabin on the Madison River. The first morning of the second week, we fished the Madison with Superflies. Every run seemed to yield two or three browns and rainbows. The fishing was so good, we found ourselves fishing the Madison every day and tying Superflies every night to replenish our supply. At the end of the week, we had caught more sixteen to twenty-three inch trout than we had ever caught. We used approximately five dozen superflies, less than one-half tank of gasoline and put less than fifty miles on our rental car.

TYING INSTRUCTIONS

Materials needed:

HOOK:	Mustad 79580 size 2 - 10
THREAD:	Camel uni-thread
LEAD WIRE:	.030
TAIL:	Brown goose or turkey biots
BODY:	Brown swannundaze (color #20 transparent brown)
UNDERBODY:	Bright yellow wool or yarn
WING CASE:	Brown turkey tail
LEGS:	Brown goose or turkey biots
ANTENNA:	Brown goose biots
THORAX:	Dubbed rabbit dyed ginger and picked

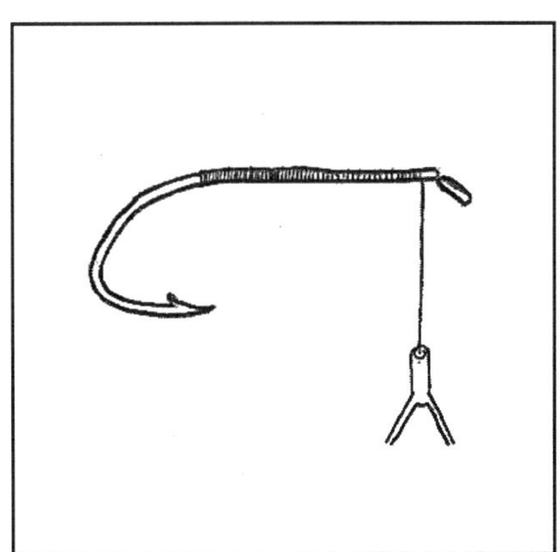

1. Place hook in vise. Starting at the eye of the hook, wind thread to the bend of the hook and back to the eye, completely covering the hook shank.

Chapter Six
Superfly

Superfly

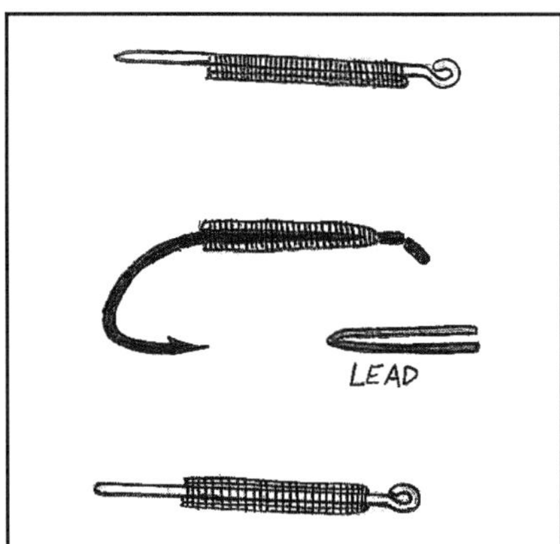

2. Fold a strip of .030 lead wire together. Place the folded lead wire along the left side of the hook. Leave approximately 1/32 inch space behind the eye and wrap thread over the wire until you reach a point approximately 1/32 inch from the back of the hook (Measure distance on a real Superfly to determine true distance.). Clip the lead wire at this point and wrap thread back to the eye of the hook. Repeat the process on the right side of the hook.

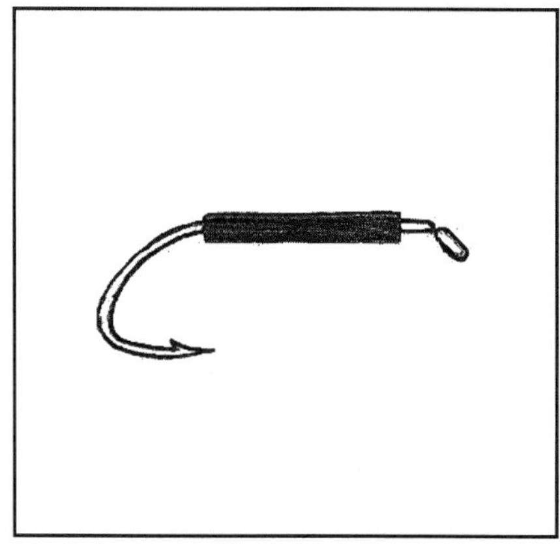

3. Wrap over the wire several times with your thread. After the wire has been securely attached to the hook as described above, lightly mash the wire and hook with long nose pliers to insure that the wire is aligned exactly with the hook and to insure that the fly will have a flat appearance. (Note: If you use regular needle nose pliers instead of fly tying pliers, you should not cut your thread with the teeth in the pliers.) Coat wire and hook with cement to insure that it bonds to the hook and will not roll.

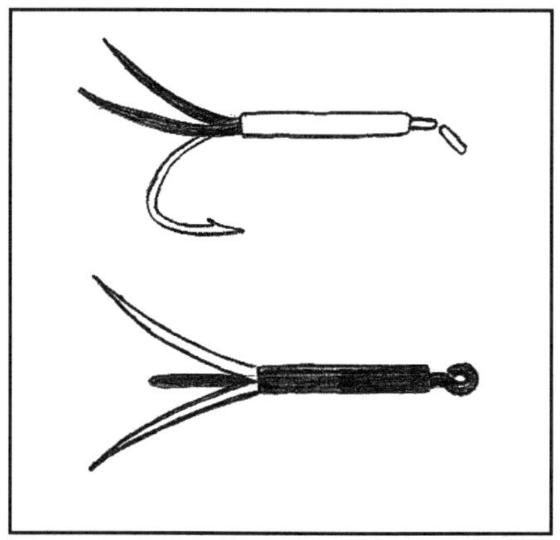

4. Cut two brown goose biots from the quill. Tie one quill on the backside of the hook to form half of the tail. Tie another biot opposite the first one. The natural curve of the biots should point away from the hook after they are tied into place.

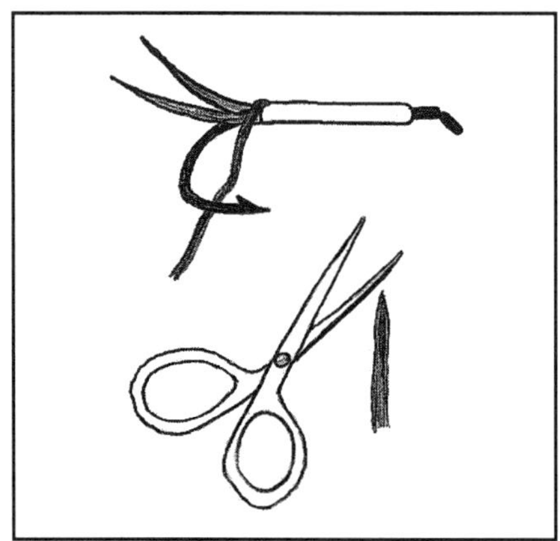

5. Clip the end of a strip of swannundaze into a point (this prevents building up too much bulk) and tie the point onto the hook in front of the biots. The swannundaze will have a flat side and a round side. Make certain the round side is facing upward, otherwise you will not obtain the segmented affect when it is wrapped on the fly.

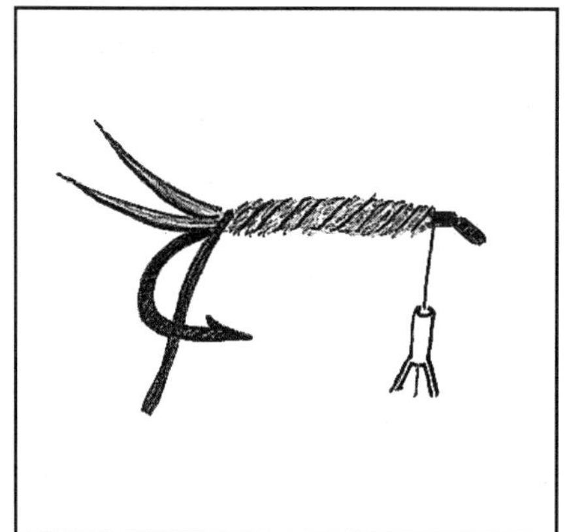

6. Wind the thread to the point where the lead ends behind the eye of the hook. At this point, tie in a piece of bright yellow wool. Wind wool over lead toward bend of hook. When you reach the end of the lead make one turn behind the lead and wind wool back to point where it was tied in. Tie off and clip wool. Wind thread back and forth over wool to securely fasten it. After this step is completed, use the pliers to flatten the wool to insure a flat appearance.

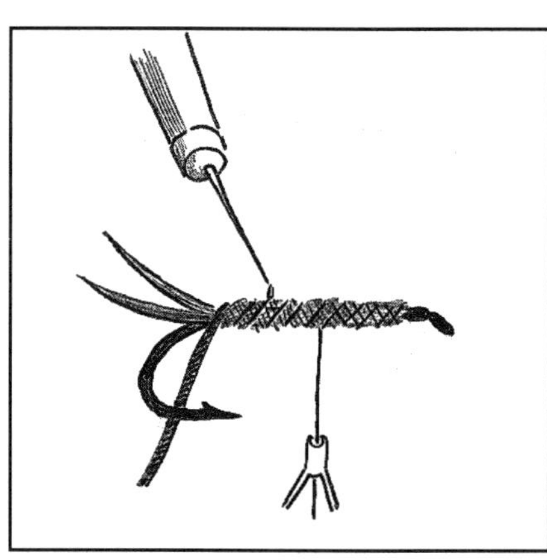

7. At the point where the swannundaze is tied in, place a drop of cement on the hook and wool. This prevents the swannundaze from slipping when it is wrapped over the wool.

Chapter Six
Superfly

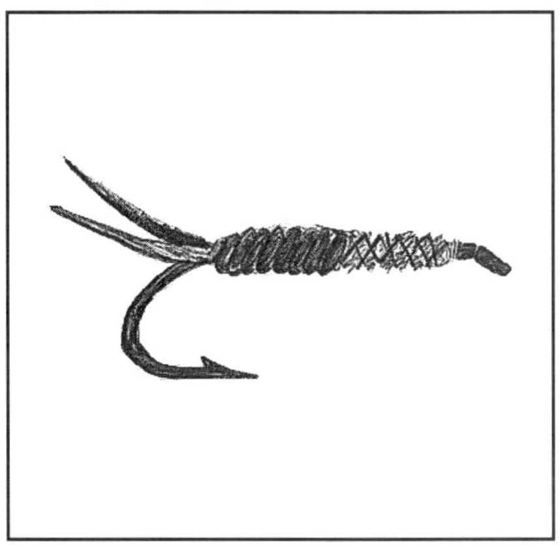

8. If the swannundaze is not wrapped on the hook and underbody properly, it will slip, causing the swannundaze to unravel. After the swannundaze has been tied into position, it will be necessary to make the first couple of turns of the swannundaze onto the hook only before covering the underbody. Make the first turn of swannundaze around the bare shank of the hook. The second turn should overlap the first turn slightly. This provides a solid base and turns the swannundaze slightly left, allowing the next turn of swannundaze to begin its climb upon the underbody. After the swannundaze begins to climb upon the wool, each turn of the swannundaze should be placed snugly against the previous turn, preventing any yellow wool from showing between wraps. Continue wraps until 1/2 of the wool body has been covered. Tie off swannundaze and clip.

9. Wind the thread back to the point where the swannundaze was clipped off. Clip a section of turkey, spray it with krylon, and tie it on top of the hook. This will be used later to form the wing case.

10. From the brown goose biot, clip two individual biots strands. The biots will have a natural curve to them. At the point where the turkey quill was attached, tie one biot on the left side of the hook. The curve of the biot should be facing you and the length should extend to the back of the body. Repeat the same process to attain the right leg.

11. Wind thread forward about 1/3 of the remaining wool underbody. a) Clip two biots to be used for legs. Match them together making sure tips of the biots are exactly even and they both curve in the same direction. b) Place the biots on top of the wool underbody with the natural curve turned upward. c) Lift legs so they form a 90 degree angle with the body. Wrap thread in front of legs several times so they will remain in this position. d) Separate the biots. Fold biot on top toward you. Make one or two turns of the thread to hold biot in this position while other leg is being tied into position. The biot should be protruding off the right side of the fly at approximately a 90 degree angle. e) Repeat the same process described in section "d" with the remaining biot. f) Using the figure-eight method, secure legs into permanent position.

Superfly

12. Wind thread another 1/3 length of the wool underbody. Repeat steps outlined under step 10. After this step, all six legs should be properly attached.

13. Remove fly, turn it upside down, and reinsert it into the vise. Wind thread back to the point where swannundaze body ends. Wax the thread with a tacky dubbing wax and dub light ginger rabbit fur onto the thread. Wrap dubbed thread around wool underbody making certain not to disturb the position of the legs. Stop after one or two turns of the dubbed thread has been placed in front of the wool underbody.

14. Remove the fly from the vise. Turn it over and reinsert it in vise. Pull the turkey quill over the back of the thorax, tie off and clip.

15. To prepare the antennae, select two small biots and tie them behind the eye of the hook. One biot should be on each side of the eye. The curve of the biot should curve away from the eye of the hook. Clip excess biot material, build up head and cement.

Chapter Six
Superfly

The French Broad River, western North Carolina. Photo by Kevin Howell.

Chapter Seven

Kevin's Stone

My son, Kevin, and I have one policy that we follow religiously concerning flies that we sell: we test every new fly pattern for durability and fish-catching ability before placing them on the market. The only time we deviated from this standard was the introduction of Kevin's Stonefly Nymph.

Kevin had been working on a new stonefly nymph for several days before settling on a pattern. After he was satisfied with his design, he tied a dozen for us to use. Before we had a chance to use them, one of our wholesale customers called to say that he was running low on flies and would take anything that we had on hand. Since we were working on several large orders and pressed for time, Kevin suggested we send him the dozen stoneflies along with some conventional patterns we had in stock.

Shortly thereafter, the wholesaler called and ordered additional Kevin's Stones stating that it was the hottest fly he carried, and that he had heard some great catches taken on the fly. This cycle of shipments and additional orders was repeated several times.

Since we were in the middle of our peak business period, we didn't get a chance to use the new pattern for several weeks. Finally, I got an opportunity to take some time to go fishing. As I left the shop, Kevin handed me two of his new flies and suggested I give them a try.

When I arrived at the stream, I began the day by using the new pattern. I wasn't overly impressed with the fly and didn't seem to take any more trout than I normally did with my standard patterns. After taking several trout, I hooked a small one, and as I was lifting him out of the water, my tippet broke. The small brown escaped with my fly. Since I was testing the new pattern, I tied on my last Kevin's Stone and continued fishing. Eventually, I hung my back cast in an overhanging branch and lost my fly. Since that was my last one, I tied on another pattern and continued to fish. Much to my surprise, the standard pattern was much less successful, and I was unable to take more than a few fish. Changing patterns several times didn't improve the situation, and I immediately developed a new respect for Kevin's new creation.

Since this initial experience, I have learned that this fly really does shine when trout are difficult to catch, and I now rate it as one of my favorites.

Chapter Seven
Kevin's Stone

TYING INSTRUCTIONS

Materials needed:

LEAD WIRE:	.015 - .025
THREAD:	Black uni-thread
HOOK:	Mustad 9671 size 8 - 12
TAIL:	Brown goose biots
ABDOMEN:	Peacock herl
BACK:	Brown turkey tail
THORAX:	Cream chenille palmered with grizzly hackle
LEGS:	Brown goose biots

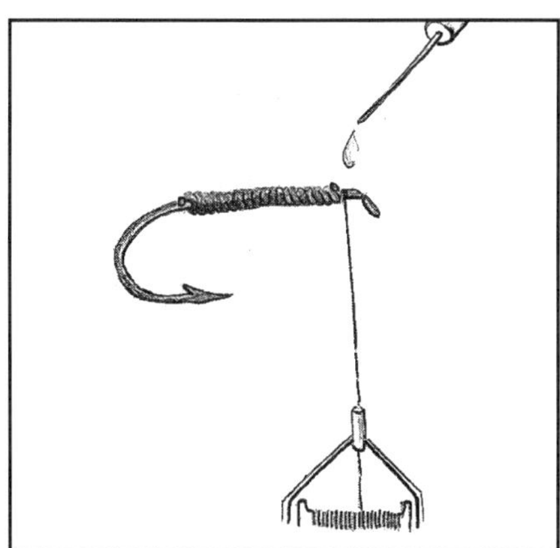

1. Insert hook in the vise and wrap shank with desired amount of lead wire. Wrap thread over lead wire to secure it to the hook. At this point, the thread should be behind the lead wire and immediately in front of the bend of the hook. Coat wire with head cement to ensure a durable body.

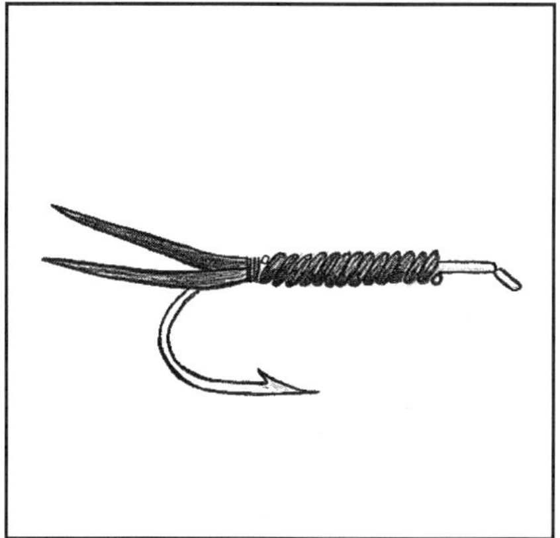

2. Wind thread to a point immediately in front of the bend of the hook. Cut two brown goose biots from a quill. Tie one quill on the backside of the hook to form half of the tail. Tie another biot opposite the first one. The natural curve of the biots should point away from the hook (after they have been tied into place). Also, the length of the tail should be approximately the same length as the shank of the hook.

Kevin's Stone

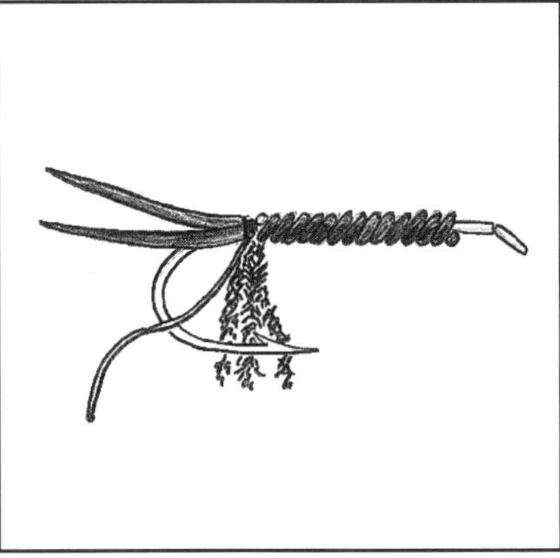

3. On top of the hook, and at the same point that biots were tied in, tie in a section of turkey tail that has been treated with Krylon. The turkey will be used to form the back and wing case for the fly.

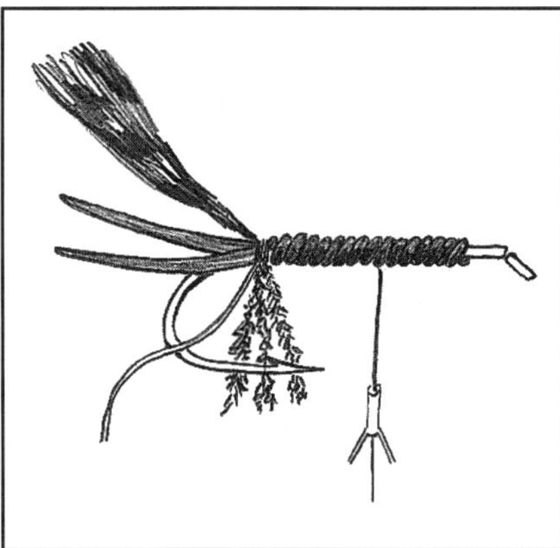

4. Depending on the size of the fly, tie in three to five strands of peacock herl. Also, at the same point, tie in a piece of size 32 gauge gold bead wire.

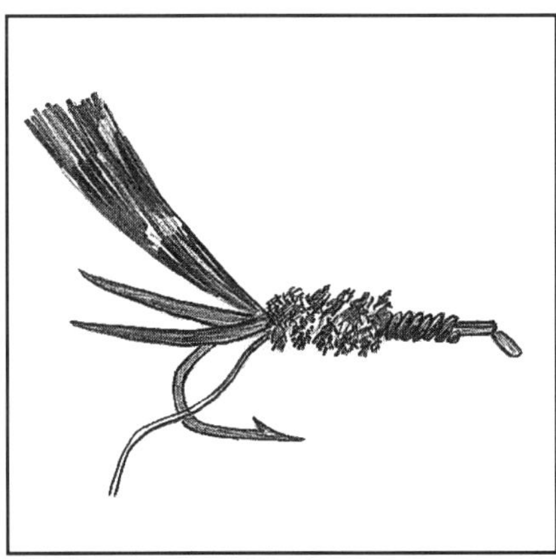

5. Wind thread to approximately the midsection of the hook shank. Wind the peacock herl up to the thread, tie off, and clip excess. To improve the durability of the fly, wind the thread back and forth through the peacock body.

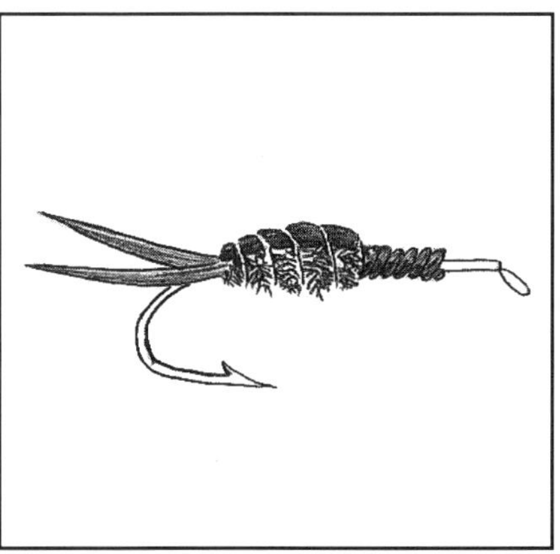

6. Pull turkey quill over the peacock body that you just formed. Do not clip excess quill as it will be used to form the wing case. Flatten the body with a pair of toothless needle nose pliers.

7. Palmer the bead wire through the body and over the top of the turkey quill, leaving a small amount of space between each turn. Clip off excess wire.

Chapter Seven
Kevin's Stone

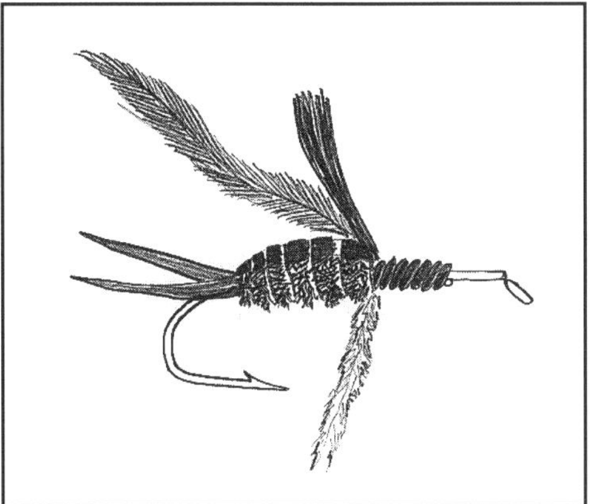

8. Immediately in front of the peacock body, tie in a piece of size medium, cream colored chenille. Also, at the same point, tie in an oversized grizzly hackle.

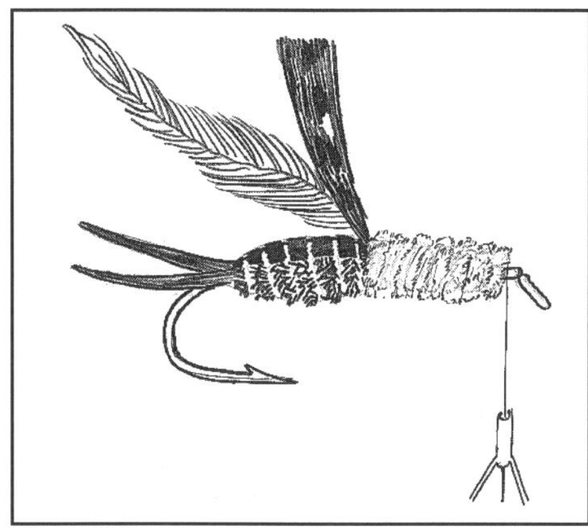

9. Wind thread to the eye of the hook. Wrap chenille toward eye of the hook, stopping approximately 1/32 inch from the eye. Tie off and clip excess. Palmer the grizzly hackle through the chenille thorax. Tie off and clip excess.

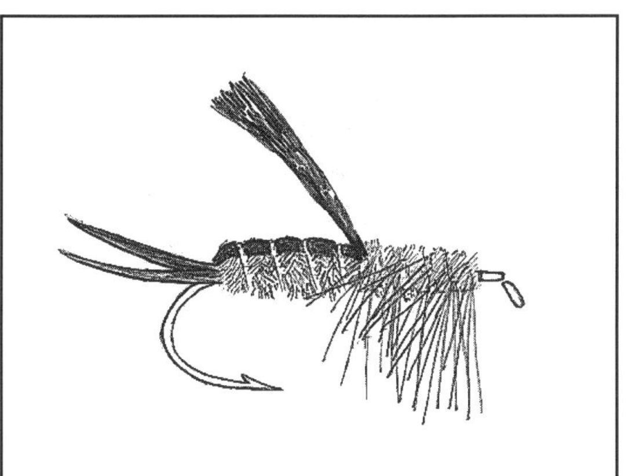

10. Remove the fly from the vise. Clip all of the grizzly hackle fibers from the top of the fly. Clip the sides and bottom to a length that equals the gap of the hook.

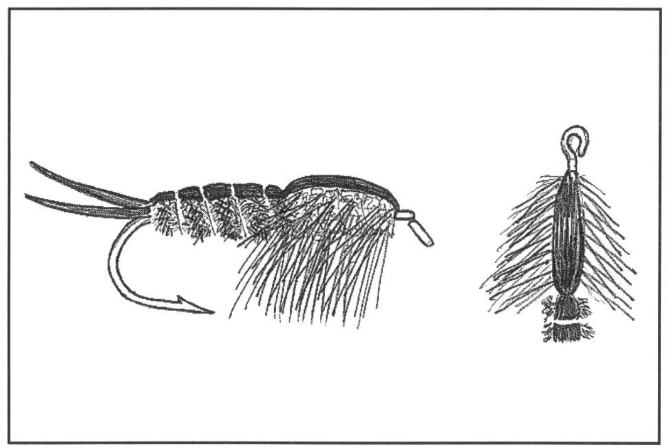

11. Replace the fly in the vise. Pull the turkey quill over the top of the thorax to form a wing case. Tie off and clip excess.

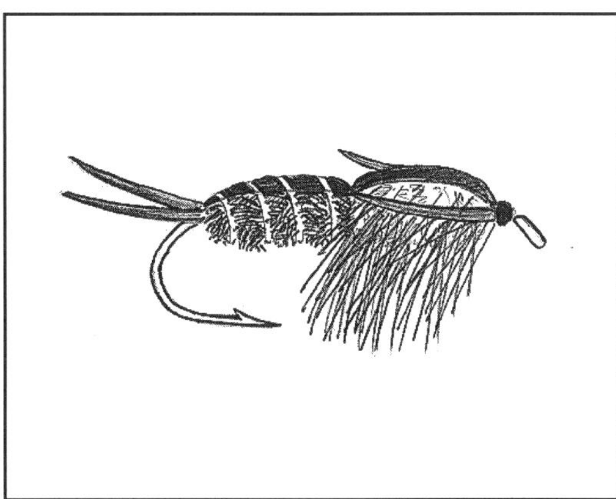

12. Clip two brown biots. The natural curve of the first biot should be facing you. Place the biot on the back side (left side for right hand tiers) and tie into position with the point of the biot facing the bend of the hook. When tied into position, the biot should extend backwards to a position equal to 1/2 of the body of the fly.

The curve of the second biot should curve away from the tier. Place this biot on the side of the hook facing you. Allow the biot to extend to 1/2 length of the body. Tie into position, build a head and cement.

Chapter Eight

Don's Pet

This is the sister-fly to the Hot Creek Special nymph, and was developed in an attempt to construct a dry fly that would be as productive as the nymph in low, clear water conditions.

After a day's fishing on the South Toe River, several of my friends and I were discussing the merits of the successful Hot Creek. During the conversation, the comment was made, "It's a shame that the Hot Creek is not a dry fly. The way it catches trout, it would be a blast to use."

This comment was all it took to get me to start experimenting at my fly-tying vise. If I could use the materials in the nymph to develop a dry fly, I could possibly have the Mother of all dry flies. Although I was unable to develop the dry fly to the same specifications as the nymph, I was able to incorporate some of the nymph's "trout-catching" materials into the fly. The results have been a very good producer in low, clear water. The iridescent sheen of the peacock body combined with the silver tinsel is a terrific fish attractor, especially when fished in sunlight.

Although the fly was developed as an attractor pattern, I've found it to be very effective when tied in large sizes and utilized during the Green Drake hatch. As a matter of fact, the largest brown taken on the pattern that I am aware of was caught by my brother, Dwight, during the Green Drake hatch.

In early April, Dwight located a huge brown in a slow moving, waist-deep, difficult-to-fish run in the Davidson River. Dwight spent every available opportunity during April and May in an effort to catch the trout, all without success. During the Green Drake hatch, the trout became very active, and Dwight reported the trout was feeding on top every afternoon. Still, he could not get her to rise to his offerings.

Late one Saturday afternoon during the peak of the hatch, Dwight and I arrived at the big trout's pool. We found a good spot along the bank and sat down to watch for signs of feeding activity. Shortly afterwards, the big trout started rising. I watched as Dwight slowly waded into position without running waves to the feeding trout. The presentation with his favorite Green Drake imitation was perfect, but the fish didn't take. After the fly floated out of the trout's window, Dwight wound in his fly, clipped it off and tied on a size eight Don's Pet.

Since Dwight was already in casting position, he didn't risk spooking the trout by wading ashore. He rested the trout by allowing her to take several

Chapter Eight
Don's Pet

drakes before he made another cast. His presentation was perfect again and the fly disappeared in a ring. A short while later, we were admiring a twenty-five inch, five pound plus hen. Another outstanding angling feat was accomplished by Dwight while using this pattern. About three years after this incident, Dwight was fishing our favorite "Big Trout" stream during the Green Drake hatch. He had heard rumors that a big brown was living in the pool he had just approached. Very cautiously, he presented the Don's Pet to the area that he felt a big trout would use as a holding and feeding area. A large trout rose almost instantly to the fly, and after several fast trips up and down the stream, he was able to net a beautiful twenty-two inch brown.

Since we fished every day during the hatch, Dwight, Ricky Hubbard (Dwight's son-in-law) and I were back on the same stream the next afternoon. Dwight and Ricky chose to fish the same section of water that Dwight fished the day before.

When they reached the pool where Dwight caught the twenty-two inch brown, Dwight turned to Ricky and jokingly said, "This is where I caught the big one yesterday. I believe I'll catch a bigger one today."

Dwight presented his Don's Pet to exactly the same spot as yesterday, and a large trout rose to the fly. After another lengthy battle, the trout tired, but Dwight realized that he had forgotten to bring a landing net. As Dwight worked the trout into the shallow water, Ricky removed his shirt, placed it behind the trout, and scooped up the trophy. This brown was exactly twenty-three inches long.

Taking two trophy, native brown trout in two consecutive afternoons, on the same fly, in the exact same spot, is an angling feat equaled by very few fishermen.

Jokingly, Dwight always said that taking these two trout was a direct result of his fishing ability. Since I developed the pattern, I always argued his success was due to Don's Pet. Regardless of the reason, Don's Pet played an important role in catching the two trophies that now sit on a piece of driftwood in Marion's (Dwight's wife) den.

Chapter Eight
Don's Pet

Don's Pet

TYING INSTRUCTIONS

Materials needed:

HOOK: Mustad 94840 size 8 - 18
THREAD: Black uni-thread 6/0
TAIL: Deer hair (from the back of an eastern whitetail)
BACK: Peacock herl
RIBBING: #10 flat silver tinsel
WINGS: teal
HACKLE: Brown and grizzly mixed

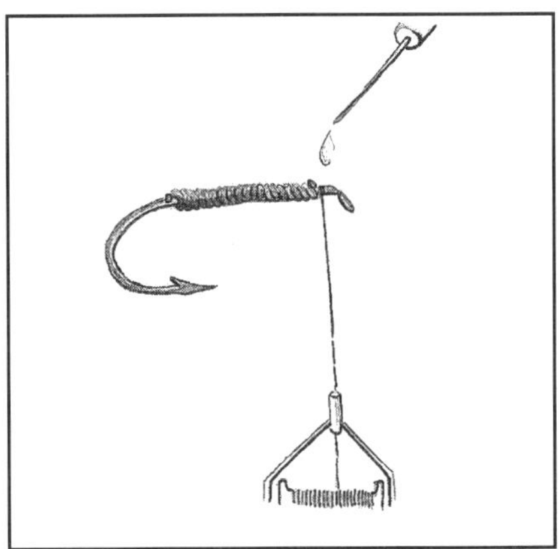

1. Insert hook and attach the thread in the middle of the hook.

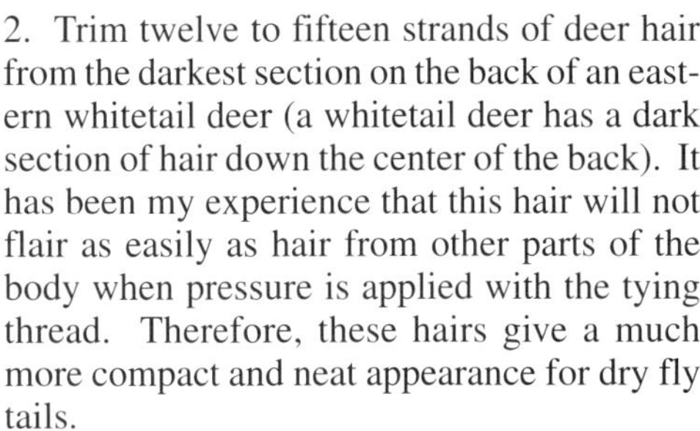

2. Trim twelve to fifteen strands of deer hair from the darkest section on the back of an eastern whitetail deer (a whitetail deer has a dark section of hair down the center of the back). It has been my experience that this hair will not flair as easily as hair from other parts of the body when pressure is applied with the tying thread. Therefore, these hairs give a much more compact and neat appearance for dry fly tails.

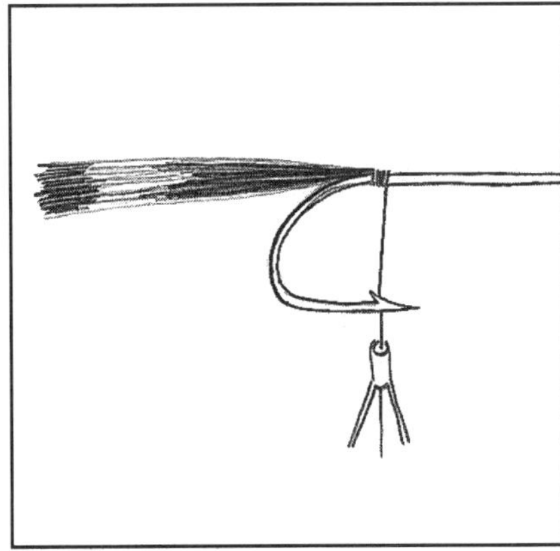

3. With thumb and index finger, work all underdubbing or fuzz out of the base of the deer hair. The underdubbing is absorbent and will soak up water, which causes the fly to sink if the underdubbing is left in the hair.

Stack the hair in the stacker to even the tips. Remove the hair and tie on the hook to form the tail. For proper appearance and balance, the tail should be one and one-half times the length of the hook shank. (Note: when using deer hair to form a tail on a dry fly, make the first couple of turns of the tying thread using extreme pressure. This will cause the hair to flare slightly. Ease up on the amount of pressure on each of the following turns as the thread is wound toward the bend of the hook. As you lighten the pressure of the turns, the thread will pull the flared hairs back together, creating a neat, compact tail.) At this point, the tail should stick straight out of the rear of the hook, and should not point up or down.

Chapter Eight
Don's Pet

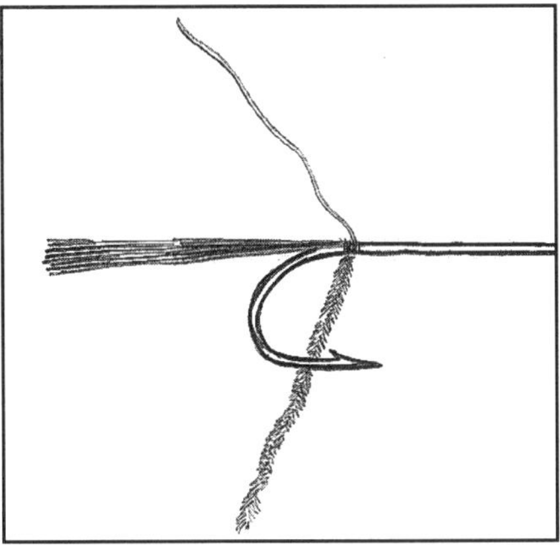

4. Immediately in front of the bend of the hook, tie in three (depending on size of hook) strands of peacock herl and one strand of size 10 flat silver tinsel.

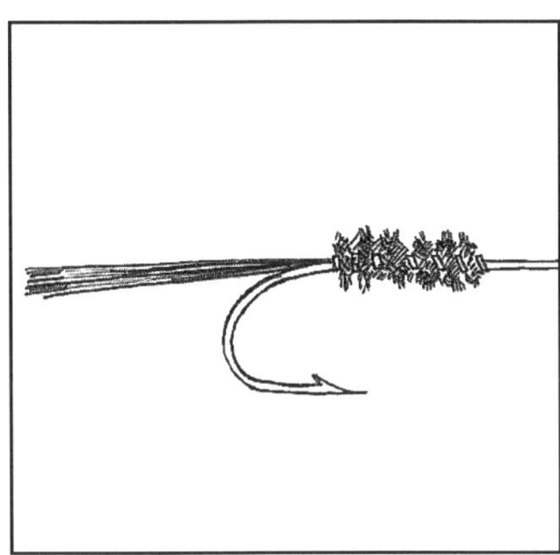

5. Wind thread toward the eye of the hook, stopping approximately 1/3 length of the hook shank from the eye. Create a body by winding the peacock herl to the point where you stopped the tying thread. Tie off excess herl and clip excess material. Wind tying thread back and forth through the body to increase the durability of the herl.

Return the thread to the point where the peacock body ends. Rib the peacock body with the silver tinsel. Tie off and clip.

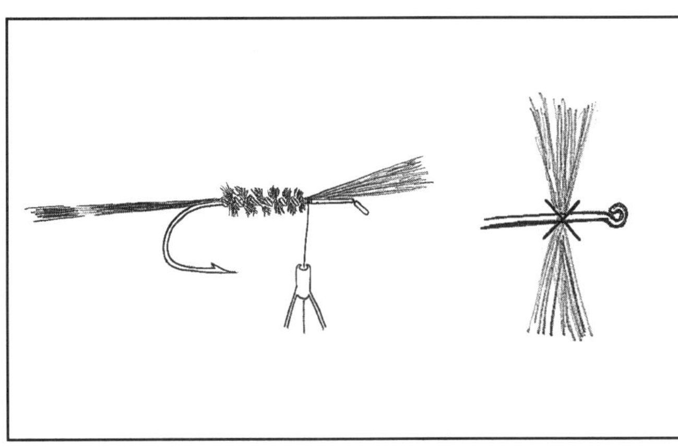

6. Select a piece of teal (mallard flank) feather to use as wings. On each side of the duck quill, cut matching portions of the fibers. In front of the body you just formed, lay the fibers on top of the hook with the tips extending over the eye of the hook. At this point, the thread should be positioned in the middle of the empty space in front of the body. Wind the thread over the fibers several times to secure them to the hook. With the index finger and thumb on your left hand, pull the fiber back until it forms a ninety-degree angle with the hook. Wind the thread in front of the fibers several times. When the feathers are released, they should remain in the ninety-degree position. Take the point of the scissors or bodkin and divide the feathers into equal parts. Using the figure-eight method, wind your thread between the two clumps of feathers. You should now have a perfect set of divided wings.

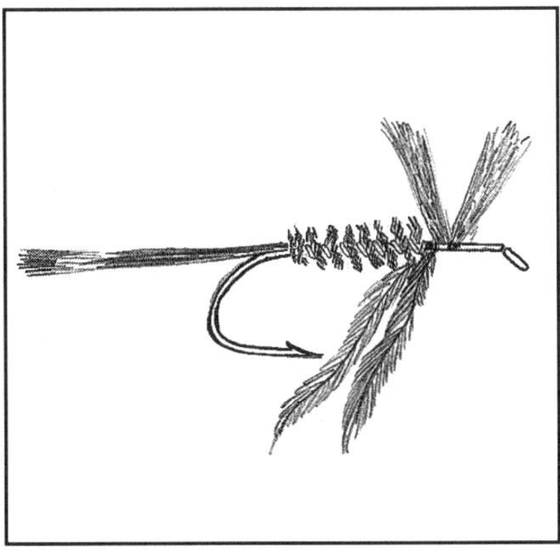

7. Wind your thread back to the front of the peacock body. Select a brown and a grizzly hackle suitable for the size hook you are using. At the butt of the hackles, clip all the "webby" fibers. Next to the body tie in the hackles and wind thread to the eye of the hook. With your hackle pliers, wind the hackles behind and in front of the wings. To ensure a pleasing appearance and balance, you should make equal number of turns of the hackle behind and in front of the wings.

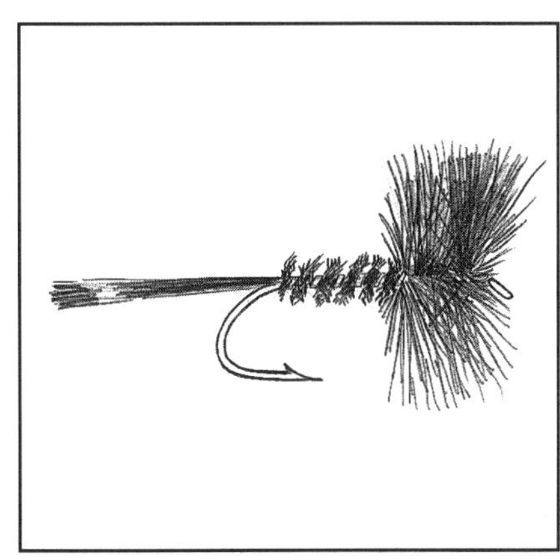

8. Whip finish and cement.

Chapter Nine

Don's Woven Nymph

I have always been intrigued by woven nymphs, although I'm sure a trout doesn't swim over to a fly, look it over, and think, "hmmm...it has a dark back and a light colored abdomen, so it must be a real nymph...I'd better eat it before it gets away." Nevertheless, using a fly constructed of two different colors gives me confidence that I can fool fish easier, because it more closely resembles the real nymph. If the angler is not confident in his fly, equipment, presentation and ability, he might as well be throwing a rock at the fish.

Although I have always had good success with woven nymphs, and I enjoy using them, I've never been very satisfied with the durability of nymphs woven from floss. After catching one or two trout, the fibers in the floss break and the fly becomes ragged, torn, and eventually, less productive. Flies woven from chenille are much more durable, but are often more bulky than I desire. Therefore, I was constantly looking for a suitable substitute for tying the woven patterns.

One day I was visiting my niece, Cindy Hubbard, who is as obsessed with cross-stitching as I am with trout fishing. During my visit, Cindy showed me a project that she had completed. I immediately recognized several colors of embroidery thread as being the same as what I used in many of the woven nymphs I tied. A switch flipped in my brain as it dawned on me that embroidery thread might be a suitable material for the woven patterns.

I tied several prototypes using the new material, and found them to be as effective, and much more durable, than the original patterns. The new material offered several advantages over conventional floss. It was not only more durable, but it was heavier, which accelerated the sink rate. Also, the material would not fray or pick on rough spots on the tier's hands. The strands could be separated into four smaller pieces, which made weaving size 16 and 18 nymphs much easier. The wide array of colors seemed endless, allowing the creativity of the tier to run wild.

Being a lover of nymphs with rubber legs, I soon added them to the new woven ones, and the Don's Woven Nymph was born.

Chapter Nine
Don's Woven Nymph

TYING INSTRUCTIONS

Materials needed:

HOOK:	Mustad 9671 size 8 - 18
TAIL:	Chartreuse rubber legs - size medium
BODY:	Top: olive embroidery thread #731
	Bottom: Yellow embroidery thread #727
WING CASE:	Black swiss straw or mottled turkey tail
THORAX:	Cream chenille
HACKLE:	Grizzly palmered through thorax
THREAD:	6/0 Lt. cahill uni-thread
WINGS:	Medium chartreuse rubber legs

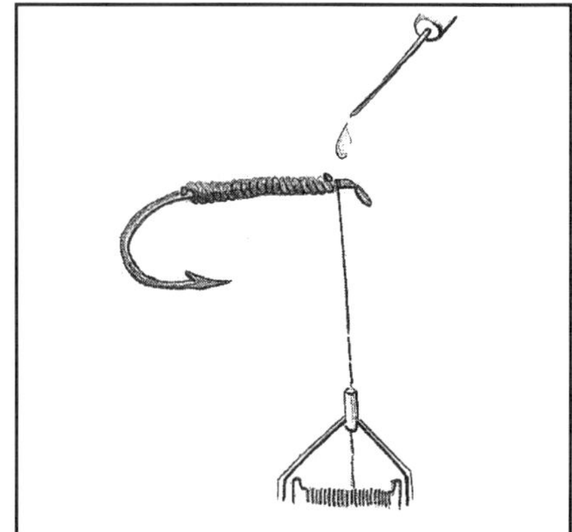

1. Insert the hook into the vise and wrap the shank with the desired amount of lead wire. Wrap thread over lead wire to secure it to the hook. To insure a strong, durable body, coat the lead and thread with fly head cement.

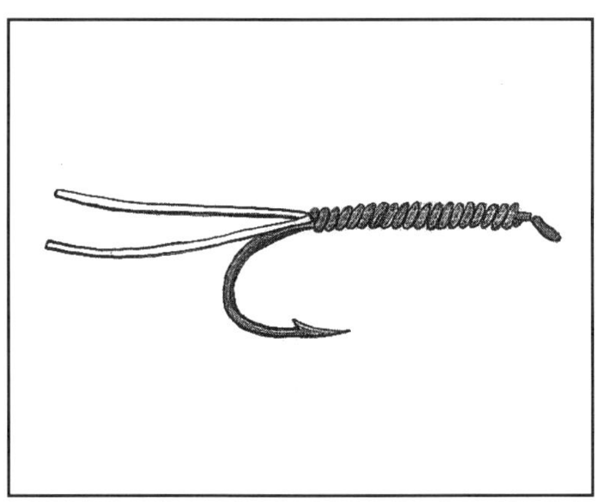

2. Cut a section, approximately one to one-and-a-half inches in length. Form a single strand of chartreuse, rubber leg material. Fold into two equal sections and place the center of the fold on top of the hook behind the lead wire. Secure legs into position with your thread. If legs are too close together, spread and use a figure-eight wrap with the thread to hold in the correct position.

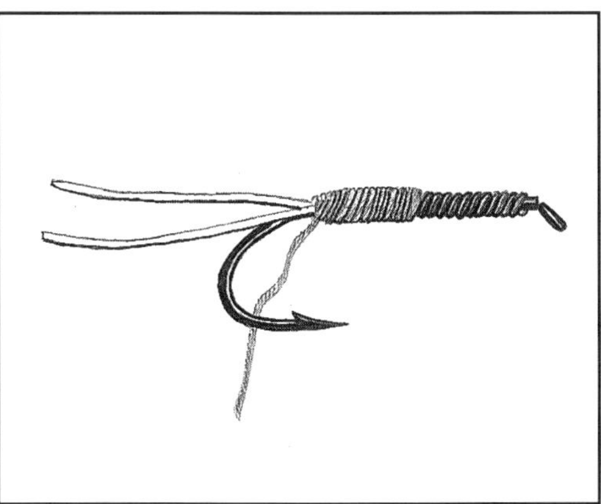

3. Wind thread to the midsection of the hook. Clip a six-inch section of embroidery thread and tie onto the hook at this point. Once the yellow embroidery thread has been tied in, wind it back to the bend of the hook where the rubber tails are attached. Wind the tying thread over the embroidery thread to the bend of the hook, and return it to the midpoint of the hook by winding forward. Make sure each turn of the embroidery thread is placed as close to the previous turn as possible without overlapping. The purpose of placing the embroidery thread in the middle of the hook and winding backwards is to build up the body and ensure a smooth, neat body. After completing the above step, the embroidery thread should be hanging off the hook on the side nearest the tier, and be positioned at the bend of the hook where the rubber tail is tied in.

Chapter Nine
Don's Woven Nymph

Don's Woven Nymph

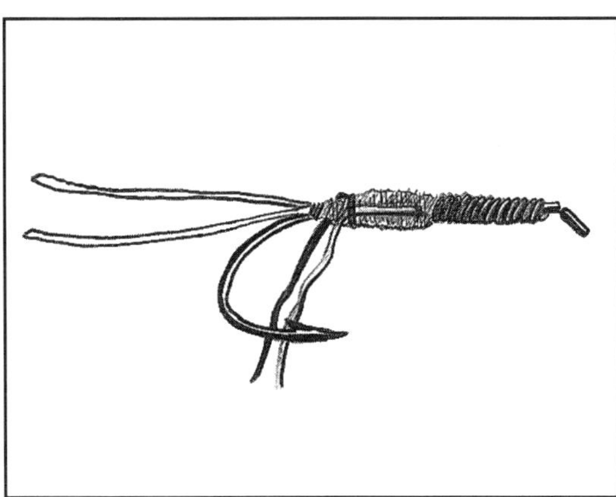

4. Cut a five inch section of olive embroidery and tie in along the opposite side of the hook (side furthermost away from the tyer.) When placing the olive thread on the hook, be sure that the end of the thread is at the point where the yellow thread was originally attached. Wind thread over olive embroidery thread to a point where the tail is attached and return tying thread to midsection of hook. After this step is completed, the yellow thread and olive thread should be exactly opposite each other, with the olive thread on the side opposite of the tier.

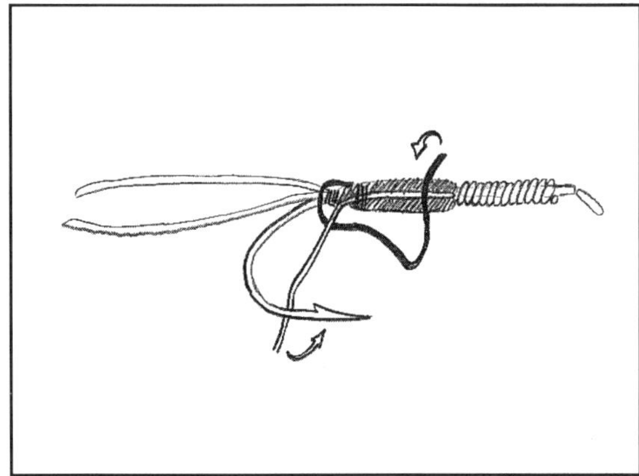

5. With your left hand, pull yellow thread toward you until it is tight. Using your right hand, pull the olive thread over the top of the hook toward you and loop or wrap it around the yellow thread. While continuing to hold the yellow thread in the position described above, pull olive thread over the back, returning it to the original side of the hook.

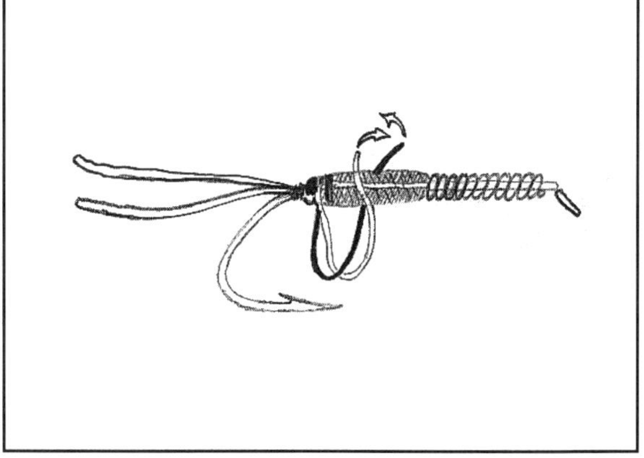

5b. Now comes the tricky part. Carefully trade hands while maintaining constant pressure on both strands of embroidery thread. With your right hand, pull yellow thread under the hook and loop it around and return it under the hook to its original position.

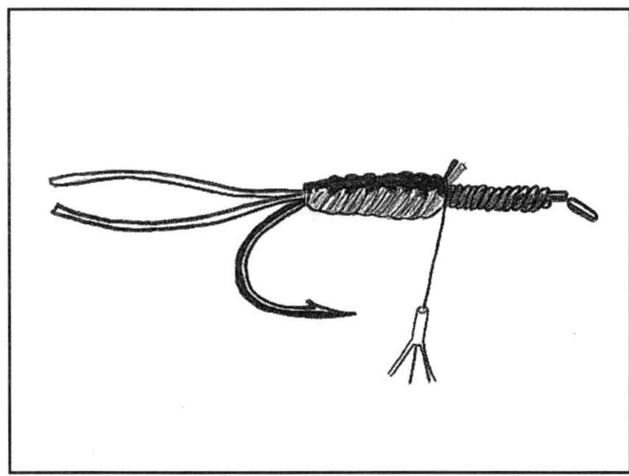

5c. Continue making the above steps until midsection of the hook is reached.

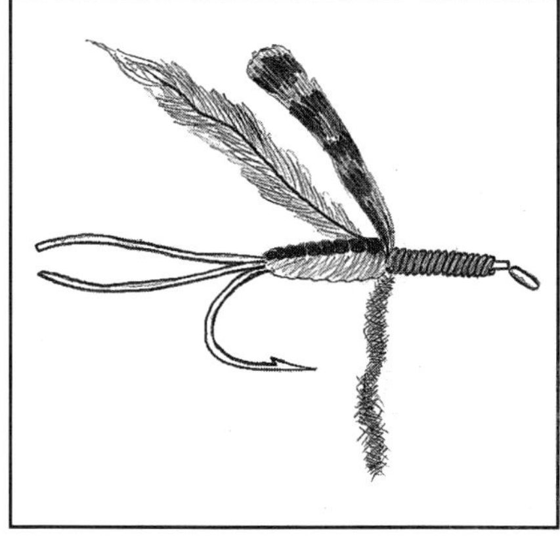

6. At the point where you end the woven body, tie in a section of Swiss straw on the top of the hook. Also at this point, tie in an oversized grizzly hackle and small piece of cream chenille. Move tying thread to the eye of the hook.

Chapter Nine
Don's Woven Nymph

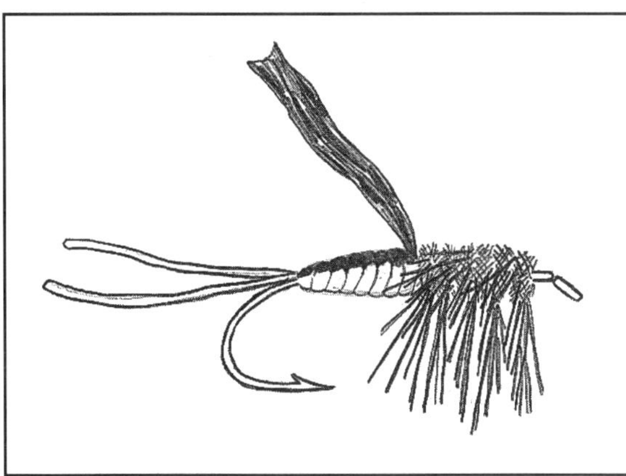

7. Wind the chenille toward the eye of the hook. Tie off and clip excess. Remember to leave a small amount of space behind the eye of the hook where the rubber legs will eventually be attached.

7b. Palmer grizzly hackle through cream chenille, tie off and clip. Remove fly from vise. Clip all hackle fibers off top of the chenille thorax you just formed. Clip all remaining grizzly hackle fibers until their length is approximately the same as the gap of the hook. On the right and left side of the hook, trim the grizzly hackle closer to the body so the rubber legs can be positioned close to the body sides.

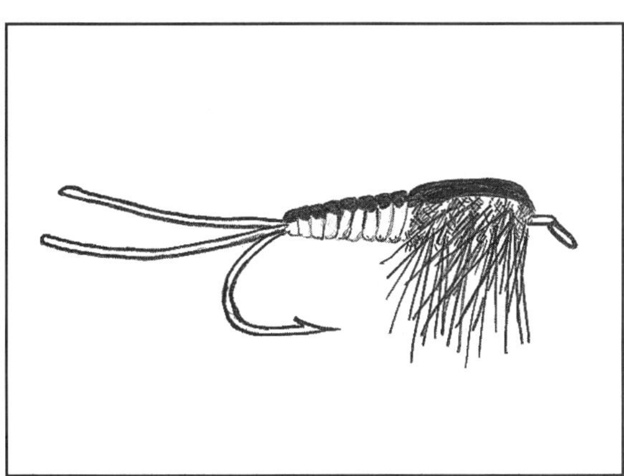

7c. Pull the Swiss straw over the cream chenille. Tie off and clip excess. Remember to leave enough room behind the eye of the hook to attach the rubber legs.

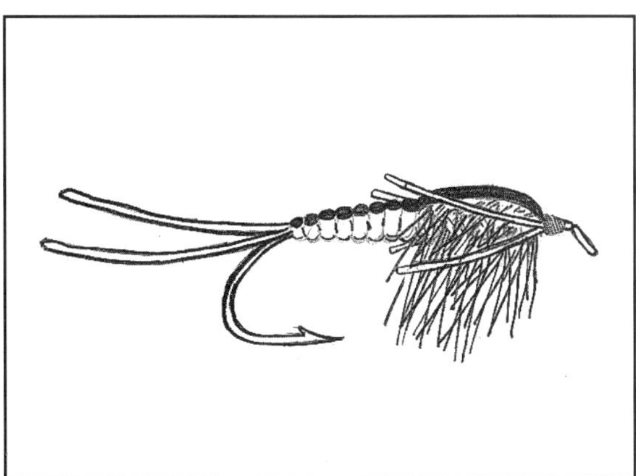

8. Select two strands of chartreuse leg material that are still together (do not separate). Cut the legs into one-and-one-half inch sections. Fold the legs in the middle. Place the legs on top of the hook just behind the eye. Using the figure-eight method (Fig. 8b. The Bug), secure the legs to the hook. After tying the legs onto the hook, they should form a ninety-degree angle with each side of the hook.

8b. With the left index finger and thumb, pull the legs back along the sides of the body. Wrap over the legs to form a head and secure the legs in position. Clip off thread and cement.

Chapter Ten

Texas Piss Ant

You're probably wondering why a Southern Appalachian trout fly is called the Texas Piss Ant. Actually, my father came up with this name due to the size of the original pattern.

Several years ago, dad hiked into Hazel Creek with brothers Dale and Jerry Hodge to enjoy several days of camping and fishing. Although Hazel Creek has a national reputation for its large population of rainbow trout, they were having difficulty catching any of them. Dale and Jerry make one or two trips into Hazel Creek each year, and had encountered these conditions before. They knew the ant they had designed would normally produce under these conditions, so they gave dad a supply to use.

When dad returned home, he was singing the praises of this new fly that would produce trout even when other standard dry flies failed. After Dwight and I got an opportunity to examine the fly, we couldn't believe what we were seeing. Due to its overgrown size, brown hackle and white wings, it really wasn't very impressive, as ant patterns go. But because dad was so impressed with the fly, we decided to tie a few to try them out.

Since Dale and Jerry always tied the pattern in size 10, we did the same. After fishing the fly, we were much more impressed with its fish-catching ability than its appearance. It truly does catch trout when other traditional patterns fail.

When trout are super-selective or refuse conventional patterns, we have found that smaller versions of the ant in size 14 and 16 are usually productive. This is true even when ants are not present on the stream and you are having difficulty determining what the trout are feeding on. Quite often I believe the trout think the pattern is a caddis due to the silhouette cast by the wing and body shape of the fly.

Several factors make this ant a terrific producer. Due to the oversized, trimmed hackle, it's a super floater. Also, the position of the poly yarn wing traps air, which assists in floating. The white wing also makes the fly prominently visible in the water, an advantage not often enjoyed by other ant patterns.

TYING INSTRUCTIONS

Materials needed:

HOOK:	Mustad 94840 size 10 - 16
BODY:	Black fly rite poly dubbing
HACKLE:	Oversized brown hackle trimmed
WING:	White poly yarn
THREAD:	6/0 Black uni-thread

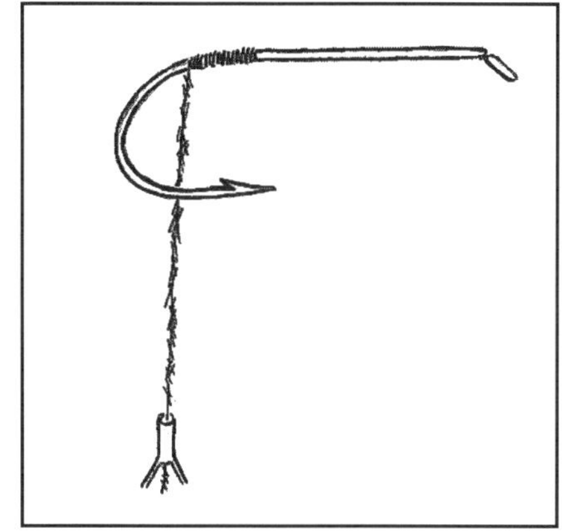

1. Attach tying thread near bend of hook. Wax thread and dub black poly onto thread.

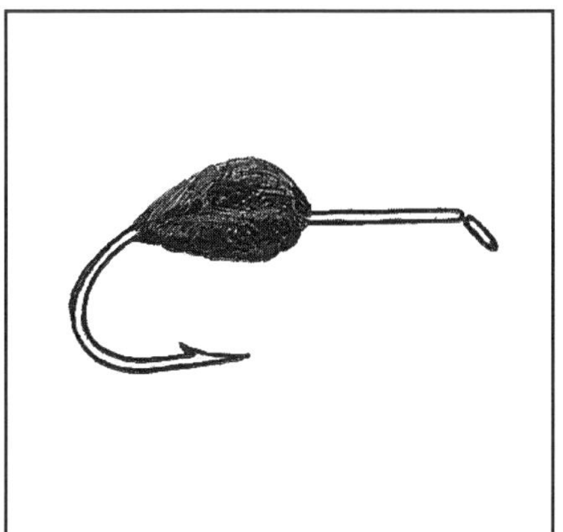

2. With the dubbed thread, create a tapered hump on one half of the hook shaft. Make certain the front and back of the hump are tapered.

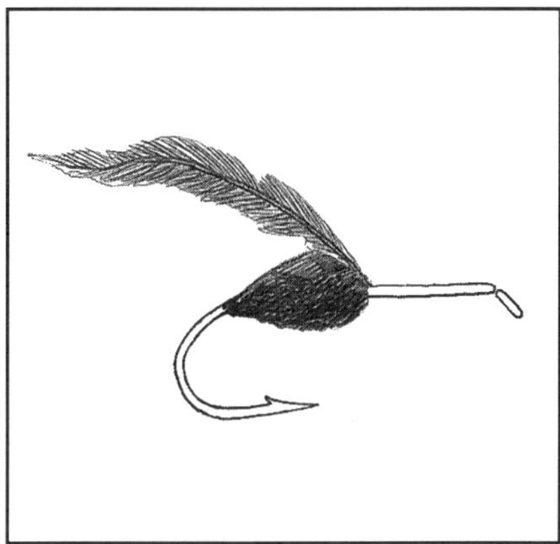

3. In front of the hump just created, tie in an oversized brown hackle. Move thread toward the eye of the hook.

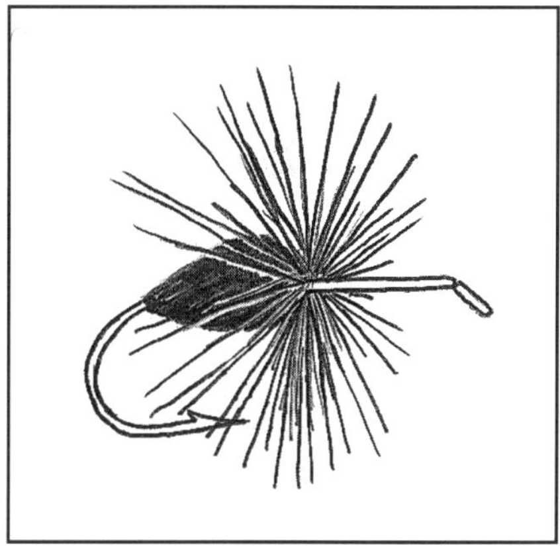

4. With the hackle pliers, make approximatley six wraps of the brown hackle around the hook. Tie off hackle and clip excess. Remove the fly from the vise and clip the hackle unit its length is the same as the gap of the hook.

5. Wax the thread again and dub black poly on the thread. Create another hump in front of the hackle. Make certain that the front of the hump is tapered. If it is not, the wing will not lay on the fly correctly.

6. Cut a section of white floating poly yarn slightly longer than the shank of the hook. If you are tying a small ant, you should remove a portion of the yarn from the strand so it will match the width of the ant's body. Lay the yarn on top of the hook and tie it down. Trim the wing so it extends slightly behind the hackle. Tie off, clip thread and cement.

Howell Family Fishing Album

Left: Don Ray Howell (age 3) and Dwight Howell (age 9) on North Carolina's Lake James.
Below: Don Ray (age 8) and Dwight (age 14) with their catch from North Carolina's Toe River.

Left: Don Ray and Dwight with their catch from North Carolina's Davidson River in 1972. Both fish are over 26" in length and weigh at least 6 lbs. Photo by Jerry McLean.

Kevin Howell on the Whitewater River, NC. Photo by A. Ruela.

Brook trout taken by Kevin Howell, 1998.

Yallar Hammer Wooly Worm

Yallar Hammer Nymph

Yallar Hammer Dry Fly

Sheepfly

Hot Creek Special

Bill's Provider

The Bug

Superfly

Kevin's Stone

Don's Pet

Don's Woven Nymph

Texas Piss Ant

Western North Carolina's Collins Creek, a typical small, technical Southern Appalachian trout stream . Photo by Kevin Howell.

Part Two

Tactics and Equipment

Chapter Twelve

Presentation

It was almost dark when my father, brother, and myself backpacked into the campsite on our favorite stream in the Smoky Mountains National Park. Upon our arrival, we discovered that three older men were already camped at the same site.

The next morning we were preparing to go fishing when the three men passed our tent carrying calcutta canes approximately ten feet in length. A three or four foot section of clear monofilament and a dry fly was tied to each cane.

Being curious about their fly fishing techniques, we secretly followed to watch. The men would crawl through the rhododendron to a likely looking spot, work their calcuttas out over the water and dabble the fly several times before dropping it on the water and allowing it to drift the length of their monofilament line. Their method proved to be very deadly on the rainbow population.

This proves that presentation is more than a long cast and the art of showing the fly in a natural manner. To be successful, the presentation must be a combination of casting, approach, reading the water, fly selection, fly design and the length and size of leader, etc. Each of these criteria are discussed separately in this book.

This discussion on presentation will not be a long, detailed lecture. You can find that in any periodical or book that has been published on the topic of fly fishing. Rather, it will be a discussion of the tricks and techniques that I feel helps to make my presentation more tempting to Mr. Lunker Trout.

Long Casts Are Unnecessary

One of the first steps in becoming proficient at presentation is to rid ourselves of the fallacies that have been received from publications and fly fishing videos. Most information concerning fly fishing stresses long casting and the importance of the double haul. Although, long, smooth casts are impressive to watch, they are completely unnecessary in most of the trout fishing that is done in Southern Appalachian streams. Most of our streams are small and choked with vegetation, inhibiting long casts.

When I was a young boy, one of my heros was Don Curry, a professional fly caster and winner of several casting tournaments. I wanted so badly to emulate those long casts, the "Snaky S", left and right curves, and double hauls. Don knew I enjoyed fly fishing and often worked with my casting technique.

Although I wasn't a very good student, I credit much of my casting ability to his instructions.

Although he was a champion caster at the time I met him, Don had never taken a trout on a fly. You're probably wondering how a "non-trout fisherman" became a professional caster. While serving during World War II, Don received a critical injury from enemy fire. He spent several months recuperating in the hospital and when he was finally able to get out of bed, the doctors suggested he start a rehabilitation program to help rebuild and strengthen his muscles. Since Don had been an avid bass fisherman all his life, it was only natural that he enroll in the fly casting class taught as part of the rehabilitation program. He quickly became adapt at casting and was soon participating in, and winning, tournaments.

Don earned a living as a chemical salesman. My father, who owned a dry cleaning establishment, was one of his customers. Before calling on my father the first time, Don had learned of my father's reputation as a fly fisherman. Since they were both avid fishermen and shared an interest in fly fishing, they soon developed a close friendship. When making sales trips to call on my father, Don always arranged his work schedule in a way that would allow he and Dad to go trout fishing in the afternoons.

I can remember the frustration and disappointment that Dad suffered after each of their fishing trips. Of the many times they fished together, the most Don caught was two, while Dad usually caught a limit, not including the ones that were released. Don, being a professional caster, always tried to fish too far in front of himself. Every trip Dad tried, without success, to convince Don to catch the trout closest to him and move to a more advantageous location to catch the ones farther upstream.

Although Dad was a super caster, he was not as proficient as Don. He was able to outfish him only because he was an expert at presentation. If Dad had not caught the trout closest to him, the trout upstream would have been spooked when the close ones panicked, then darted upstream to seek cover.

In addition, Dad had better control of his line and fly by making the shorter cast. Long casts usually encounter several different currents, each trying to pull the fly line and fly

Don Ray Howell with a 6 lb. brown caught on North Carolina's Elk River in 1997. Photo by Zane Howell.

Chapter Twelve
Presentation

in different directions. A natural drag-free drift is almost impossible to achieve under these circumstances.

Because of Dad's frustrating experience with Don, he always insisted that I concentrate on presentation, casting accuracy and approach rather than long distance casting. Although I admired Don's casting ability, I was fortunate to be mature enough to analyze the situation and determine that successful trout fishermen are not necessarily expert long distance casters. This point was dramatically illustrated by the fishermen using calcutta canes rather than expensive fly rods.

Presenting Dry Flies to Visible Trout

All of us have seen it. A lunker in the lower end of a pool suspended a few inches under the surface, lazily fanning, waiting for an unsuspecting bug to float close enough to become the next meal. The natural first thought is, "This is too good to be true! If I can cast in front of the trout and get a natural drift, catching him will be as simple as taking candy from a baby." Unfortunately, this is WRONG!

Presenting the fly in front of the fish is the worst presentation that can be made. It allows the trout an increased amount of time to inspect the fake bug as it floats toward him. The longer he looks at it, the more convinced he becomes that his dinner tonight will not include a chunk of steel and a feather. In addition, it allows the trout an opportunity to see at least a small portion of the tippet. Most trout have master's degree in bug identification and they know most natural flies do not have strings attached. In the words of my father, "This causes a refusal on behalf of the trout."

The most productive presentation is to cast the fly behind the fish and slightly to one side. The trout will see the movement as the fly settles on the water and turn to inhale it without hesitation. By placing the fly behind the trout, it cuts down on the amount of inspection time. He knows the fly is floating out of the pool and he must get it before it is swept away. Also, since the trout will approach the fly from behind, he will be unable to see the tippet as easily.

This type of presentation calls for extreme accuracy in casting. The fly should never be presented higher than the midsection of the trout. If the fly lands directly over the trout's head, he spooks or at least becomes suspicious of the overhead activity. Also, the fly must be presented slightly to the side which allows easier detection of movement by the trout. A less than perfect cast usually results in a no-catch situation.

Chapter Twelve
Presentation

Presenting Nymphs to Visible Trout

The big disadvantage of presenting a nymph to a visible trout is that the nymph, unlike the dry fly, must be presented in front of the trout in order for the nymph to sink to the proper depth before reaching the trout.

This type of presentation calls for two special tactics on behalf of the angler. First, the nymph, especially if weighted, must be presented in a manner that allows it to settle softly into the water. A big, heavy nymph falling from the heavens is something that trout are unaccustomed to, and causes undue suspicion.

Secondly, the nymph must be cast far enough in front of the trout to ensure that it will be at the same depth as the trout when it drifts into position. If the nymph is cast too far upstream, it sinks too deep and will be below the trout's feeding lane when it drifts into position. Trout will move up to take a nymph but will rarely go down to catch a drifting nymph. This is probably due to the fact that trout have difficulty seeing directly below themselves.

About ten years ago I was fishing one of my favorite streams when I spotted an eighteen inch brown suspended off the bottom. After presenting a fly approximately ten times, I figured the trout had gotten wise to my presentations. Out of pure stubbornness, I presented the fly one more time. For some reason unknown to me, I began making a series of short twitches as the nymph approached the trout. Immediately the trout charged the nymph and inhaled it completely. Since that initial experience, the "twitching technique" has produced many nice trout that refused the conventional method.

When the nymph is twitched it gives the trout the illusion that it is struggling to reach the surface or is trying to escape being eaten. Regardless of the trout's "thoughts", it is a technique that proves to be deadly on suspended trout that refuse conventional presentations.

One word of caution: the series of twitches must be very soft and gentle. Long, hard twitches must appear unnatural, as it rarely produces a strike.

Avoid Casting Too Quickly

A feeding trout moves into a position that allows him to hold in the current without too much difficulty, and one that moves a great deal of food into striking distance. When the trout spots food, he darts out of his holding position, inhales the food, and returns to his holding position. Sometimes, rather than darting out and catching the food, the trout will float downstream slightly in front of the food, inspecting the bug before opening his mouth and allowing it to float in.

Chapter Twelve
Presentation

By casting to the rise immediately, the angler increases the possibility of spooking the fish. If the fish has not moved back into the original holding position when the fly is cast, the possibility of casting the line or leader over the fish is greatly increased. Also, a cautious trout will usually not feed again until he returns to his previous ambush point to make sure his environment is safe and secure. Therefore, if he sees the offering before he is in position, he will not strike.

Some trout, especially large ones, feed very methodically. They rise to a fly, allow two or three to float by without taking them, then take the next one that drifts into position. By presenting the fly before the trout is ready to feed, the angler is allowing the trout extra time to inspect the offering, which increases the possibility of leader detection or recognizing the fly as a fake. The angler should observe the trout for a few minutes to determine the cycle and present the fly at the exact time the trout is expected to feed.

All of us miss trout as they rise to dry flies. The trout either recognize the fly as an imitation in the last split second before it is inhaled, or the angler strikes too quickly, jerking the fly away from the trout. Either situation causes the trout to become very nervous and suspicious. The angler should allow the trout to calm down before presenting the fly again.

If I miss a relatively small trout, I make three to four casts to other areas in the stream that cannot be detected by the trout. I will then begin casting back to the one I missed. This will usually be enough time to allow the trout to overcome suspicion and revert to the feeding mode.

When I miss a trophy fish, I employ a little different tactic. Usually, I will quietly wade ashore and take a seat on the bank where I can watch the area where the trout struck. If a hatch is present and the trout begins to feed again, I will allow him to take three or four flies before I move back into position and cast to him again.

If no hatch is present, I allow the trout to rest for a minimum of thirty minutes before presenting my fly to him again. I have a close friend who has the policy of smoking a cigarette before repeating a cast to a big fish he missed. It doesn't matter how you spend your time - the important thing is to allow the trout to resume feeding and feeling comfortable and secure before presenting another fake offering.

Strange things can happen when resting trophy fish. Other fishermen often blunder into the pool and frighten the fish. Once a squirrel dropped a hickory nut out of a tree into the water, spooking a trophy of approximately five pounds.

Recently, I spotted a trout of approximately seven pounds. When I presented my nymph to her, she swam over to it, looked it over, then returned to her hold-

Chapter Twelve
Presentation

ing station. I decided to rest her for thirty minutes before casting again. I waded ashore and took a seat, all the while watching the trout as she fanned slowly beneath the surface. Suddenly she spooked and swam rapidly to cover at the head of the pool. I was trying to figure out what had gone wrong when a voice blurted out, "Caught any fish?" When I looked up, a man and woman, dressed in solid white, were standing on the bridge that spanned the river. Upset, I left the pool, and my only consolation was that I knew where a big trout lived. Maybe I would get another chance before someone caught her on bait or hardware.

Cast Where Others Don't

Southern Appalachian anglers are faced with a presentation problem that does not affect anglers in other parts of the country - rhododendron. Rhododendron not only provides shade, cover and security for trout, but is also a pain in the rear end for the angler struggling to cast beneath it's choking limbs. Reluctantly, I am going to share a simple secret that will allow easy access to the water beneath rhododendron limbs, as well as other types of overhanging vegetation.

If I spot a trout, or even suspect a trophy trout might live beneath a clump of rhododendron that cannot be penetrated with a cast, I simply wade over to the rhododendron and clip one or two small branches with my pocket knife, creating a very, very small opening. I do not want to make the opening too noticeable to other anglers and I certainly don't want to make it easy for them to cast to a trophy trout that I have located. The next time I'm on the stream, I can cast my fly through the opening and present it to fish that haven't seen very many imitations. This technique calls for extreme accuracy in casting. The opening that I've created is usually only large enough to allow the leader and fly to pass through.

Careful observation on behalf of the angler is another method of improving presentation. The angler should constantly be watching for pockets, runs, and hiding areas that are not fished by other anglers.

Several years ago, Dwight and I took "Cap" Weise into South Mills River. After arriving at the river, we split up with the understanding that we would meet back at a certain pool at noon to have lunch. When lunch was finished, Cap decided to fish the pool where we had lunch. Dwight and I watched as Cap fished. When Cap finished fishing the pool, Dwight asked to borrow Cap's rod. Dwight then proceeded to wade into the pool, and cast his nymph into a hidden pocket that Cap had not fished. On that first cast, Dwight caught a nice brown.

Chapter Twelve
Presentation

Dwight returned the rod and Cap continued to fish upstream as Dwight and I followed along the shore. When Cap finished fishing the next pool, Dwight again asked to borrow the rod. He proceeded to repeat the same procedure, and once again caught another nice brown.

Cap was an expert at reading water, but he had become careless. I can certainly remember his embarrassment at missing those fish, and Dwight's joy in catching them behind him. The incident was cause for a long running joke between them. Every time they were fishing on the same stream, Dwight would always ask Cap if he could fish behind him so that he could catch Cap's rejects.

The point I'm trying to make is that anglers must be observant at all times. Even experienced, expert anglers can overlook potential fish-producing areas by being careless. By not being observant, many inexperienced anglers fish where they should wade and wade where they should fish.

Don Ray and Dwight Howell in 1984. Photo courtesy of the Transylvania Times.

Chapter Twelve
Presentation

Presenting the Fly at Different Angles

Natural barriers such as large boulders, deep water and overhanging branches often dictate how the fly is presented to the trout. If, for example, unnavigable deep water and a sheer rock bluff exists on the left side of a pool, anglers will be forced to present the fly from the right side of the stream. After several anglers present flies from this position, the trout become accustomed to that presentation and quickly learn that flies presented in this matter are to be avoided. Trout become so accustomed to this presentation that an offering from any other angle will automatically draw a strike. Therefore, anytime I encounter a natural presentation barrier, I work as hard as possible to overcome that obstacle and present my fly from the opposite side.

Several years ago I was fishing with my good friend Alex Schenck from Flat Rock, NC. Alex fished this stream on a regular basis and knew where several large trout lived. As we separated to fish different sections of the stream, Alex told me where an extremely large trout was located. He said several people had seen it on a regular basis, but no one had been able to entice her into striking.

When I arrived at the pool Alex had described, I noticed a very steep bank on the left side of the stream. A large hemlock with overhanging branches was growing on the bank. In addition, this bank was lined with large, rugged boulders and jagged stones which made walking and standing virtually impossible. Between the right shore and the area on the left where the trout held were numerous strong currents which made a drag free presentation from the right impossible.

After analyzing the situation, I decided that the only possible way to catch the trout was to present the fly from the left side of the stream. I walked several hundred yards downstream and crossed to the left side. By wading water that reached to the top of my waders (not recommended) and scaling rocks that required me to be half-monkey, I managed to work into casting position on the left side of the pool.

In spite of my unbalanced and awkward position, I managed to make a perfect cast with my nymph into the trout's holding area. When the line hesitated slightly, I set the hook sharply and felt a large fish shake her head. Line screamed from the reel as the trout made a tremendous run upstream. Because of my dangerous position, I was unable to follow the trout. Eventually I felt the line go limp as the trout evidently got slack and as far as I know, the trophy of a lifetime is still swimming in that stream.

Later that afternoon, I recounted the story to Alex. He wanted to know if that was an old Indian trick. Everyone he knew was afraid to approach the pool from the left fearing they might fall and injure themselves. The point is, you must decide if the risk is worth the opportunity of taking a trophy trout on a fly. Fear of injury is one reason I usually fish with someone else. We normally take turns maneuvering into risky presentation positions, so that the one not fishing can keep a watchful eye on the one taking the risks.

Unusual Presentations Are Sometimes the Most Effective

My son, Kevin, turned to me and said, "Dad, is that big fish a trout?" After I slowly slipped into position beside Kevin, I could see the big fish, a brown trout of approximately seven pounds, fanning slowly two feet below the surface. Kevin was using a dry fly and I told him to cast to the trout. His cast was perfect, slightly behind the trout and off to one side. The trout didn't move and completely ignored the cast, acting as if she hadn't even seen the fly. His second cast was again perfect, but the trout once more ignored the presentation. At this point Kevin suggested I try a nymph.

As the nymph drifted to the trout, she swam to it and I braced for the expected strike. Without taking the nymph, she slowly turned and swam back to her original position. Quietly, we waded ashore where I tied on a new, lighter tippet and changed nymphs. After approximately thirty minutes, I returned to casting position and presented the nymph again. Once more, the trout reacted in exactly the same manner. She swam to the nymph, inspected it, and returned to her holding position.

The entire process was repeated once again. I waited another thirty minutes, again changed nymphs and tippet, and presented the nymph. Yet again the trout looked at the fly and returned to her holding area. By now I was becoming discouraged, so I began changing nymphs without resting the trout between presentation. Each time I showed her a new nymph she reacted the same way. I kept changing nymphs until she had seen almost every pattern in my fly box. Each time her reaction was the same.

While looking for a different nymph, my eyes fell upon an extremely large hellgrammite pattern that I had tied to use in heavy, discolored water. The hellgrammite was tied on a size 4, 6x long hook and weighted extremely heavy. My thought was, "If I can't catch her, I might as well scare her," so I tied the hellgrammite on and made a cast. It appeared as if a rock had been thrown in on top of the trout when the nymph hit the water. Before the nymph could sink to the trout's level, she charged the hellgrammite and inhaled it.

Chapter Twelve
Presentation

When I set the hook, she shook her head and started to bolt out of the pool when the fly came out of her mouth. Since I thought the trout would not strike, I had made the mistake of tying the fly on the light tippet; therefore, I subconsciously told myself not to strike too hard or the leader would break. Evidently my strike was so light it didn't bury the heavy hook into her mouth and another trophy sank into the darkness of the pool never to be seen again.

After many hours of thought and meditation, I've never been able to rationalize a reason for the trout hitting the heavy, oversized fly. Something about the appearance of the fly or the awkward presentation rang the dinner bell for her, proving that fish are not always susceptible to conventional presentations. Possibly, she struck the fly out of aggravation or irritation from having so many flies thrown at her.

One of the most unusual presentations I ever used occurred while fishing for Arctic Char in Alaska. My brother, myself and four of our friends were spending a week at Painter Creek Lodge. Tired from several days of catching twenty-five to forty pound King Salmon, we decided to spend one day fishing for Char.

We were flown by bush plane to a small stream called Featherly Creek, which was about a ten minute flight from the lodge. When we arrived at the stream, we were instructed by our guide to use egg patterns, wooly buggers, or streamers. We were told to cast the patterns above the fish, allow them to drift to the fish, and be prepared to set the hook, because the char would take the fly every time.

The stream was absolutely choked with char and every run and pool seemed to be lined with them. In some pools we counted as many as fifty. This seemed too easy. Catching them would be like shooting ducks on a pond, but after fishing approximately a mile and a half, we could only account for two or three small char. They were completely oblivious to our flies, even allowing the flies to brush against them without making any attempt to strike or spook.

Disgusted, we decided to return to the lodge and fish a stream that had provided lots of action from the Kings. The only way back to the plane was to wade downstream. Fish in this stream see very few people and as a result they don't spook very easily. We could actually wade within a few feet of them before they slowly moved out of the way. As we were wading downstream, I nonchalantly cast my egg pattern in front of and above a fish. Since I didn't have much line out, the fly swung toward the char and stopped several inches in front of him. The fish raced upstream and struck the egg pattern. After releasing the fish, I tried the same tactic again and caught another fish. My buddies started imitating me and seemed to catch a fish on every cast. You would not have believed the number of sixteen to twenty-eight inch char we caught that afternoon.

Chapter Twelve
Presentation

Most anglers (and all fish) know that it is not natural for salmon eggs to drift downstream, stop and remain completely motionless in the current. However, this unnatural presentation was a killer on that particular day, proving once again that the unconventional is sometimes the most productive.

Can you imagine a limit of ten native brown trout that range in size from sixteen to twenty-two inches? I saw such a limit! What's really hard to believe is they were caught by a novice that had very little experience using a fly rod and had *never* been trout fishing in his life. This angler was from Florida, and came to western North Carolina for several weeks of vacation. While in North Carolina, he decided to try his hand at trout fishing. When inquiring about a stream to fish, someone suggested he try the Cane River, located in Yancy County, North Carolina.

The only equipment the gentleman had was an old, dilapidated fly rod and a few small popping bugs that he used for bream fishing. The popping bugs were tied to a single section of eight pound monofilament which he was using for a leader. Because of his inexperience and the heavy stream vegetation, he was unable to make conventional casts. After several futile attempts at casting, he decided to alter his presentation by fishing downstream. Somehow he was able to lob the popping bugs into the water in front of himself. Once the popping bug was in the water, he would allow the current to carry it downstream until his line was tight. When all the slack was out of his line, he would hold the popping bug in position allowing the current to bounce it up and down. For some unknown reason, every large trout in the stream fell victim to this most unconventional presentation.

If someone had told me this story, I would have probably accused them of lying, but I know the story is true because I was also fishing that day and met the old gentleman on the stream. He showed me his fish and demonstrated the method he had used to catch them. I don't remember catching very much that day, but believe me, I was really impressed by his success, and I've tried this method several times - always without success.

One other unusual catch stands out in my mind. My father and I were at our favorite pool on Linville River in Avery County, N.C. Dad had fished the pool carefully, making several good presentations with his dry fly, but was unable to entice a trout. Since it was almost dark and we had arranged for our friend Hughes Burleson to pick us up at the bridge, Dad suggested we stop fishing and wade upstream to the bridge. Because we were no longer fishing, we were pretty careless with our wading. We sounded much like two Evinrude outboard motors going upstream, as we were running large waves over the pool. As we waded, Dad had about four feet of line hanging off his rod and was dragging his fly on the water beside us. A fifteen inch brown came up through the waves and

Chapter Twelve
Presentation

noise, taking the fly almost beneath our feet.

These stories sound unbelievable, but they are true and I hope they do more than entertain you. They certainly prove that trout don't read the same books and articles that we do, and that trout sometimes don't react in the way experts say they will. Hopefully, these stories will encourage you not to get into a rut, and when conventional methods are not producing, you will not be afraid to experiment. Don't hesitate to use extremely oversized flies in clear water. Also give your flies action, create a false hatch, or try any other screwball, unconventional presentation that you can think of. If conventional methods are not producing, it certainly won't hurt if you try the unconventional. Just keep in mind the possible rewards.

Some Common Presentation Mistakes

During my guiding experiences, I've seen novice fishermen catch trout on terribly sloppy casts, though any cast that produces a trout is considered to be perfect as far as most anglers are concerned. Most experienced fishermen fail to realize this concept.

When experienced anglers make unsatisfactory casts, they immediately lift the line off the water and repeat the cast, attempting to correct the mistake. It's almost impossible to lift the line off the water without creating some unnatural movement or disturbance, which causes trout to scurry for cover. The best way to correct a poor cast is to allow the fly and line to float completely out of the trout's window where the disturbance cannot be detected. In addition to preventing the trout from detecting the movement, allowing the cast to float will sometimes produce a fish, thus making the imperfect cast perfect.

Evidently some anglers enjoy casting more than fishing. They cast a dry fly to a likely looking spot and immediately pick up the cast and make another. The only fish they catch are the ones that are aggressively feeding. Most trophy trout are deliberate feeders and rise slowly, examining the offering thoroughly before inhaling the fly. By making the cast too fast, the angler is taking the fly away from slower feeders, as well as increasing the possibility of spooking the trout by lifting the line and fly off the water too frequently.

Earlier, I stated that it is not necessary to be a long distance caster in order to be a successful fly fisherman. Although long distance casting is not necessary, accuracy in casting is an ABSOLUTE must. The fly MUST be presented to exactly the right feeding spot, without showing unnatural fly line, leader, or drag to the feeding trout. Sometimes this involves unconventional or trick-casting techniques.

Chapter Twelve
Presentation

The natural casting pattern for right-hand anglers is to allow the rod and fly line to flow over the right shoulder. This allows for perfect casting to the angler's left side and directly upstream. Occasionally, when wading on the right side of the stream, the natural casting pattern is interrupted due to natural obstructions such as overhanging bushes, deep water, rock cliffs, or a combination of these factors.

When standing on the right side of the stream and trying to cast to the left, if the normal back cast is hampered due to obstacles, the natural casting pattern must be changed. While facing upstream, the angler should place the rod in front of his chest and allow the back cast to flow over the left shoulder during the cast. The angler should use the same rhythm and aiming procedure as normally would be used. It's not a difficult cast, but as with any type of casting, it does require practice, and it does pay big dividends by adding several fish to your bag per year - one of which could be a trophy.

A couple of my buddies take a lot of ridicule from me because they will not learn to make this cast. When they encounter a situation as described above, they simply turn around and begin making false casts as if they were going to cast downstream. After making several false casts, they simply allow one of the back casts to drop into the water. I think you are smart enough to know that their accuracy is not very good and their method does not produce very many fish.

Accuracy - it's the most important part of presentation. Without it you'll never be a truly successful fly fisherman, and unlike horseshoes and hand grenades, close is never good enough. Practice, practice, and practice again until you can drop your fly into a tea cup on almost every cast. Your reward will be the smelly, wiggly creatures that add so much pleasure to outdoor experiences.

Another common mistake I see, even among some experienced anglers, is the way the rod is positioned while nymph fishing. Rather than taking up slack line as the nymph drifts downstream, the rod is held at an extremely high position to help lift the line off the water to prevent drag. As the line drifts downstream, the rod is slowly lifted until it reaches an extreme of about ninety degrees to the water. With the rod in this position, it's extremely difficult to set the hook when the strike occurs.

If the angler strikes with the rod in the ninety degree angle, it is difficult to move enough slack line to ensure a firm hookup and the fish will usually throw the hook after a few runs. Dropping the rod into the normal position and taking up slack before setting the hook usually allows enough time for the trout to spit out the nymph before the hook set. Either method results in a no win situation.

Chapter Twelve
Presentation

After making a long cast with a nymph, I usually position my rod slightly higher than a forty-five degree angle and slowly pull excess line through the guides with my left hand as the nymph drifts downstream. When a strike occurs, my line will be tight and a tremendous amount of line can be moved as the rod tip is lifted in an upward motion driving the hook deep into the fish's mouth.

Kevin Howell with a 19" brown trout taken with a Kevin's Caddis Fly, September 1997.

Chapter Thirteen

Observation

My obsession for catching large trout is so great that I spend as much, if not more, time searching for large fish as I do actually fishing. When the family plans outings such as Sunday afternoon rides, picnics, hiking and camping trips, I try to arrange for these activities to occur near productive streams so I can spend a portion of my time observing the stream and specific pools that have been rumored to harbor trophies.

It was on such a family outing that I located the third largest trout I had ever seen. My wife and I were on a Sunday afternoon ride in the Davidson River area when I decided to stop and check some pools. When I slipped to the first pool, I saw a twenty-four inch brown holding in a rock crevice in the middle of the pool. Since I didn't have fishing gear with me, I told my wife I would return Wednesday morning (the stream was open to fishing only on Wednesdays, Saturdays and Sundays) to fish for the trout.

The next Wednesday morning I had parked my car and was getting my gear prepared just as daylight was breaking. As I approached the pool, I got on my hands and knees and crawled through the rhododendron to the edge of the pool. I was really disappointed when I didn't see the large trout I had located earlier in the week. Since the fish wasn't present, I decided to wait and watch the pool in case she decided to move into feeding position. After waiting about an hour, I realized the fish wasn't going to show, so I decided to fish the pool and head home.

I entered the stream well below the pool and slowly worked into casting position. Before making a cast, I checked the pool again. Still, no lunker was present. Just as I started to make a cast, a movement under a large rock on my left caught my eye. It was the trout I had spotted earlier. She was swimming slowly out from under a large rock toward the center of the pool. Instead of stopping in the crevice where I had spotted her earlier, she swam in a circle around the pool and back under the rock.

I waited and shortly she reappeared, repeating the same trip. The trout made three trips under the rock. On the third trip out, another trout, much larger than the first, followed. Both trout made the same trip through the pool. When the smaller trout reappeared, the larger one wasn't with her. This time the smaller trout swam to the rock crevice and stopped. I nervously waited but the larger fish never reappeared. As my nymph washed into the crevice, the trout took it. After a terrific battle, I landed a twenty-four and one quarter inch brown.

Chapter Thirteen
Observation

The trout that had followed her earlier was tremendous in size. He dwarfed the one I had just caught and appeared at least twice as large.

After telling my brother Dwight about my experience, we made a vow to catch the trout. The rest of the summer was spent observing and fishing for him. He was very cautious and his actions made him extremely difficult to fish for, much less catch. Late in the afternoons, he would slowly swim out from under the rocks, cruise thorough the pool two or three times, then return to his hiding place. In the many hours that we spent fishing and watching him, we never saw him feed, and he never attempted to strike our flies.

When deer season opened in the fall, we heard rumors about deer hunters shooting a large trout in the pool where the monster (which we had named "Long Thomas") lived. One rumor indicated he was thirty-three inches long while another one reported him as thirty-six inches. Regardless of which was correct, he was an awesome fish and certainly did not deserve to die in this fashion.

Friends who are aware that I spend many hours observing a stream often ask what I look for when attempting to spot a trophy trout. As crazy as it sounds, I don't look for the entire fish - very rarely can the entire fish be spotted. Therefore, I look for flashes of the fish's side, movement, different colored objects, and shadows of the fish on the stream bottom. In addition, trout have certain habits and features which give their location away.

One telltale feature is the fish's mouth. When large trout are resting they work their mouths slowly much like a cow chewing its cud. This chewing motion causes the white in their mouth to show, making them easy to spot against dark bottoms or stream shadows. When the angler spots a small white movement, it may take several minutes of observation before the fish's form can be put together with the movement.

Another feature that reveals a fish's location is its shape. Most rocks in a stream are worn round from years and years of water flowing over them. Since trout are not round, it is relatively easy to pick out their contrasting long, parallel shaped bodies against the rocks. True, you will occasionally pick out logs, sticks, and other debris, but your ability to identify contrasting shapes is an asset that will put mounted trophies on your wall.

Chapter Thirteen
Observation

Locate One - Locate More

Locating a specific fish pays bigger dividends than providing an opportunity to fish for, and possibly catch, a single trophy. Once a large fish is located, you have possibly located an area that will produce other trophies in the future. There are only a limited amount of pools and runs in a given stream that provides the food, feeding lanes, and oxygen needed to sustain a large trout. Therefore, if you catch a large fish and the stream produces large numbers of big fish, another trout is likely to move into the exact same spot. Also, quite often two or more large trout will live together in the same pool.

I once found a lunker "honey hole" in the Davidson River. The water flowed rather swift into the head of the pool, washed against an undercut bank, smoothed out, and then flowed into the next pool. About midway in the pool was a bright, sunken orange colored rock. The rock wasn't particularly impressive, as it didn't stand out of the water, wasn't very noticeable by anglers, wasn't very large, and didn't have a shelf that would hide a fish. Over a seven year period, though, I caught one rainbow and four brown over twenty-two inches in length next to that rock.

Evidently, this rock was located where the greatest amount of food washed during high water, because all five fish were caught on large Bitch Creek nymphs in high water conditions, and every one of them struck the fly in exactly the same location. The undercut bank evidently provided necessary cover and the fish would move to the rock when they had a desire to feed.

You can imagine the sick feeling I had in my stomach when I went to the pool and the rock was gone. During that fall we had an extremely hard rain which caused serious flooding and rearranged my pool. Although the pool still looks productive, I've never taken a decent trout from it since.

If a large trout is taken from a spot, another lunker may not move in immediately, but the spot will always be a potential lunker home as long as the course of the stream is not altered. This is especially true if the stream is not extremely productive.

A good example of this occurred several years ago when my brother was fishing a small stream that was known to produce some large fish, but not an abundance of them. In a particular run he hooked a tremendous brown and fought it for several minutes before breaking his line. Twenty years later, I hooked and lost another tremendous trout in the exact same location.

Chapter Thirteen
Observation

Locating is No Guarantee for Catching

The prerequisite to catching a trophy trout on a fly, especially nymphs and dries, is to find the fish in shallow water, in a feeding mood, and secure in his environment.

Regardless of how hungry the fish may be, or how long it has been since he fed, he will not feed consistently until confident he is safe from predators. That is the reason that after coming out of hiding most large trout will cruise the pool several times to check the surrounding conditions before settling into a favorite feeding lane. As long as he is cruising, it is almost impossible to entice him into striking.

From observation, I've concluded that trout engage in two types of cruising. As mentioned earlier, they cruise for security reasons. Other times they cruise in search of food. When cruising for food, they are much more vulnerable to a well-presented fly. If they are cruising for security, it is almost impossible to entice them into striking. That is the reason I always observe a cruising fish for several minutes before presenting my fly.

Most feeding fish will usually settle into a feeding mode after two or three trips through the pool, but not always. Fish, like humans, do no always act in a predictable manner. As a matter of fact, after many, many hours of observing large trout, it has become apparent that each has a different personality or behavioral pattern. The behavioral pattern of some fish makes it impossible to fish for, or catch, the trout. I will never forget the behavioral pattern of a seven pound brown that Dwight and I named "Roving Injun Joe". Joe lived under an extremely large boulder in the middle of a large pool. Each afternoon just before dark, Joe would slip out of his home and cruise or "rove" the pool. If a hatch was occurring, he would take three flies off the surface as he cruised and then return to his hiding spot.

In the three years we fished for Joe, we never saw him eat any more or less than three flies, and he never fed from an established feeding lane. Because of his insecurity with his environment and constant roving, it was extremely difficult to present the fly in a natural and tempting manner.

Evidently, "Roving Injun Joe" died of old age, because he is no longer in the pool and I never heard of him being caught. "Long Thomas", mentioned earlier in this chapter, also had a unique personality. He would come out of hiding late in the afternoon and cruise the pool, but never fed before returning home. The moral of the story is that regardless of the number of large trout you locate, they are difficult or impossible to catch if they are psychos and do not conform to trout norms.

Chapter Fourteeen

Locating Trophy Trout

My wife and daughter accuse me of being obsessed. They're right! I am obsessed - obsessed with fly tying, deer hunting, catching stripers on top water lures, bass fishing, and the biggest obsession of all - catching twenty-inch plus, deep bodied, brown trout on flies.

To be consistent at catching trophy trout, you must know where the lunker lives, where he hides, where his feeding lanes are, and when he is most likely to feed. The most obvious step in locating a lunker trout is to locate a stream that has a reputation for producing trophies. Most streams will yield an occasional lunker, but the angler will reap larger benefits by concentrating on the streams that produce large numbers of trophy fish.

After talking to game wardens and taxidermists, and checking state record books to determine productive streams, the task of locating a specific lunker begins.

Fishing Methods that Locate Lunkers

Several years ago, my father devised a super system for locating trophy trout that we call the "golden bullet". When the streams were extremely low and clear during the hot summer months, Dad would tie a size 3, single blade, gold Hildebrandt spinner trailed by a yellow canary fly to his conventional fly fishing outfit. The rod he used was usually an eight to nine footer and the leader ranged from six to seven and one-half feet in length. The spinner was unweighted, and he didn't add additional weight to the leader.

To present the spinner, he would use a sidearm cast whenever possible. This cast allows the spinner to hit the water at an angle that causes it to skip much like a flat stone. Once the cast had skipped to its destination and entered the water, he would sweep his rod to the right as hard as he could to begin a very, very fast retrieve. Since the spinner was not allowed to sink very much, the fast retrieve would often cause the spinner to break the surface of the water.

According to Dad, the two most important aspects of this method were the fast retrieve and the skipping of the spinner. He felt that the spinner skipping across the surface on the cast as well as the retrieve gave the illusion of a minnow being chased by another big fish. When one fish sees another one feeding, he usually wants in on the action and will begin to hunt forage also. It is the

Chapter Fourteen
Locating Trophy
Trout

same principle as throwing one grain of fish food into the hatchery pond, or when a bass or striper chases a school of shad to the surface. When one fish races forward and grabs the food, he is soon joined by all his friends in the area. By using the spinner to create an illusion of a frightened bait fish about to be eaten by another fish, you have turned on your prey's instinct to feed.

You are probably wondering just *how fast* is a fast retrieve. If you could have watched Dad's retrieve, your first impression would have been that a trout couldn't catch anything moving that fast. His theory was that the movement and sound of the spinner had created the illusion of fleeing bait fish as well as the desire to feed. He did not want the fish to get a very good look at the spinner because it would be recognized as a fake. Also, the fast moving lure drew instinctive strikes from the fish. The fish either grabbed the supersonic bait without thinking or it would be gone forever.

If you are not a diehard fly fisherman who is offended by catching large fish on hardware, this method offers you two advantages. Many trout will follow the lure back to the angler, while others will inhale it. Either way, the angler has located his lunker.

Since I've never been very excited about catching fish on hardware, I remove the fly from my spinner. This prevents hooking or catching the fish. I'm not sure if this system would be legal in our fly fishing-only streams since technically I'm not fishing. Rather than challenging our laws, I use different tactics when searching for trophies in restricted streams.

Using Skaters to Locate Lunkers

One good method of locating fish in these restricted waters is to use a skater. The skater is an extremely oversized dry fly that resembles a bi-visible. It is called a skater because the angler pulls the fly across the water, causing it to skate or dance. This dancing sensation is very effective in drawing strikes from oversized fish. Unfortunately, trout are extremely difficult to hook on the skater because the thick, oversize hackles act as a weed guard, allowing the fly to be jerked out of the fish's mouth without burying the hook into the flesh. Skater fishing requires some modification in equipment. The skater should be used on a seven-and-one-half foot knotless leader. The short leader turns the air-resistant fly over much easier than longer leaders and it eliminates the wake that is created by knots on conventional tapered leaders as the fly is pulled or danced across the surface.

Chapter Fourteen
Locating Trophy
Trout

It is very important that the skater float on the tips of the hackle. Otherwise, it has a tendency to dip or dive underwater as it is pulled. To ensure proper floatation, I rub silicone line dressing into the fly, making certain the hackle tips are treated thoroughly. If the skater becomes waterlogged after catching a fish or after constant use, I make several false casts to remove excess water, then place the fly into a powdered fly dry solution. Shake off excess powder by tapping it against the reel and re-treat with silicone line dressing. If the fly does not float properly after this treatment, it will be replaced with a new one. Since we are talking about proper floatation, the skaters should be carried in a box that will not crush the hackle tips. If the hackles are crushed, it is impossible to obtain proper floatation.

A slight modification in fishing technique will be required when skater fishing. When the skater is cast into a still pool, it should be allowed to float momentarily before beginning a series of short pulls or jerks. The pulls should be a very slow, gentle and soft lifting of the rod. If the fly is floating properly, the pulls will induce an erratic action and the fly will give the appearance of "tip toeing" across the surface.

In swift runs, the fishing technique is much the same as using conventional dry flies. After the skater is cast to a likely-looking spot, it should be allowed to drift without imparting any additional action (the current will provide this), causing the fly to act erratically. Also, adding action while the fly is floating in swift water will cause it to sink.

The most difficult modification to learn is the proper method of setting the hook. As stated earlier, it is difficult to hook fish because of the fly's hackle. Therefore, when a fish takes the fly, allow a small amount of time to lapse before setting the hook. This allows the fish to get the fly into his mouth and clamp down on it. Usually I say, "I hope you got it, ole boy" before setting the hook. Believe me, it is much easier to talk about *not* setting the hook instantly than it is to do it.

Waiting to set the hook will not ensure a hook-up, but it will improve your percentage slightly. The majority of the strikes will be missed, but that doesn't matter because you have accomplished your goal of locating an oversized fish that can be caught later on a different pattern.

Skaters are usually not available in most fly shops. Therefore, I will describe the tying procedure. Normally, the hook is a short shank, turned-up eye model, and the fly is a very simple pattern to tie. It does not have a tail, body, or wings, and is constructed by palmering hackles around the shank of the hook. The only difficult step is finding proper feathers.

Chapter Fourteen
Locating Trophy Trout

To provide proper floatation, the feather must be extremely stiff, oversized and web free. There are only a half dozen or less suitable feathers on a hackle. These feathers are called spade hackles, and grow on the throat of a chicken. Therefore, a few of the feathers can sometimes be located on each side of a commercially prepared hackle.

Once proper feathers have been located, they should be plucked from the hackle and trimmed to remove webs from the butt of the stem. After trimming, tie the butt of three or four hackles in front of the bend of the hook. Using the hackle pliers, wind the feathers over the hook shank, tie off at the eye of the hook and cement. When the fly is finished, it should be approximately the size of a silver dollar.

Don Ray displaying a fly tied by his good friend, Bill Hale. Courtesy of the Transylvania Times.

Chapter Fifteen

Big Trout, Flies and Muddy Water

As "Cap" Weise stepped onto the porch of the lodge, he peered over at me and demanded, "What are you doing sitting here? Daylight is burning and it's the best time to fish it has been in a month." I had always respected Cap's ability to catch trout and his knowledge of their habits. I was, however, beginning to feel that he had been fishing in the hot sun too long and lost his ability to reason clearly.

Cap, myself, and several of our friends had been invited to fish at an exclusive, private fishing lodge in North Carolina where the trout are protected by *catch-and-release* and by *fly fishing-only* regulations. This and a supplementary feeding program not only produced large populations of trout, but some very, very large trophies as well.

Unfortunately, a severe thunderstorm arrived at the lodge at the same time I did. The result was that the stream rose rapidly and became very discolored. Since I was limited in the amount of time I could fish, I sat on the porch, understandably disgusted. I was surprised when Cap said that this was a good time to fish. Jokingly, I told him that I didn't bring any garden hackles with me. "You don't need worms," he replied. "I'll let everyone know that I'm here, I'll get my waders on, and we'll go after that lunker."

When we arrived at our chosen location, Cap sat down on the bank, then proceeded to cut his tippet off, along with several more inches of his tapered leader. He replaced it with a section of strong, six pound monofilament. When Cap finished modifying his leader, it was approximately the same length as his eight foot fly rod. He explained that a long leader is unnecessary since heavy nymphs are cast a very short distance and the fish are not very spooky in this type of fishing.

After leader modification, he selected a big (size 4) solid black, heavily weighted nymph and waded into casting position. Cap started making a series of very short casts into the foaming water which poured into the head of the pool. After the fly was cast, he would allow it to sink momentarily and would hold a tight line as the fly drifted past him. His casts were not much longer than his rod. On approximately the tenth cast he set the hook on a beautiful sixteen inch rainbow. After releasing the trout, he waded back to the same location, repeated the process, and released two more trout before giving up on the run.

Chapter Fifteen
Big Trout, Flies and Muddy Water

During this entire process, I was standing on the bank looking like a big-eyed boy at a picnic, simply amazed that trout could be caught on flies in muddy water. Cap was eager to help me rig my outfit (and to coach me) as we turned the "rained out" trip into a productive day's fishing. Not only did I enjoy a great day fishing, but I learned a method that has enabled me to catch more trophy trout than any other method I have ever tried.

After a thunderstorm, big trout take the opportunity to gorge on food washed into the stream. They use the security and protection of the discolored water much like the darkness of the night. Though the trout have moved from their protective homes in deep water into the shallows, they still behave with a feeling of security and protection. Thus, they are much more susceptible and vulnerable to your fly.

Large trout are normally lazy creatures, and during these conditions, they will go where they can catch the most food without expending a large amount of energy. The best places to find them are the heads of pools where swift, foamy water carries food from upstream, at the bottom of pools where the food gathers before washing downstream, or other locations in pools where the current captures the greatest amount of food and washes it into one central location.

In order to be successful, you must not only select the correct location, but you must be willing to change your normal fly fishing style slightly. In addition to using a shorter, stronger leader, you must move at a much slower pace, making many repeated casts to the same spot. Repeated casts are necessary because the trout's visibility will be much lower in the dingy water; therefore, it may be necessary to present the fly many times before he sees it. It is not unusual for me to make twenty-five to seventy-five casts into a location that I feel may be holding a lunker.

Some years ago, I was fishing one of my favorite streams when a sudden storm muddied the water. A couple of years before, my son, Kevin, and I had located two very large trout that lived in a large pool not far from where I was fishing. Quickly, I hurried to the pool, modified my equipment and began fishing. From past experiences, I knew exactly where the fish's feeding lane was located and I began making repeated casts to this spot. After about fifty casts, I I was ready to give up. On my last cast, I felt a fish take. Upon setting the hook, I realized that I had hooked one of the largest trout that I had ever seen.

I've taken several large trout, all species of salmon up to forty-plus pounds, large northern pike, large and smallmouth bass, and many other species on a fly rod, but having this huge trout hooked was the first time I ever felt completely helpless with a fly rod.

Chapter Fifteen Big Trout, Flies and Muddy Water

The trout fought an unusual battle, never attempting any extremely fast, hard runs or attempting to go under the rock ledge at the head of the pool, easily cutting the tippet. Often he turned his tail toward the surface and appeared to be standing on his head as he rubbed his mouth on the bottom, trying to rid himself of the fly. As he tired, he would simply swim to the bottom of the deepest portion of the pool and sull until he was rested, then repeat the process again. As he sulled, it was impossible to move him, although I threw rocks into the water above him, thumped the rod butt, and waded as close to him as possible, kicking the water to create a loud disturbance.

I am reluctant to reveal (because most people think I'm lying) that it took one-and-one-half hours to tire the fish. Finally, he turned on his side and I was able to work him into shallow water. As I removed my net from the retriever and was preparing to net him, he rolled slightly and the fly popped out of his mouth. He was so tired that he wobbled slowly into the depths of the pool.

Unfortunately, I've never seen the fish again and I fear that the long battle might have killed him. Approximately a year later, I was lucky enough to catch his mate. She was thirty inches long and weighted exactly ten pounds. The fish I lost was considerably larger than the one I caught and I estimate that he was in the twelve-to-fourteen pound range.

Since this is a big fish method, I try to have several trophy fish located before the season starts so I can devote all of my "thunderstorm fishing" exclusively to these fish. Once I've located some trophies and conditions get right, my family and friends know the only place they will be able to find me is on the stream. It's the one time I drop everything I'm doing, regardless of its importance, and spend as much time as possible fishing. During this time I figure my chances of catching a trophy has been increased about 200%.

If I'm unable to locate trophy fish, I devote my fishing time to pools where I've taken large fish in the past, or pools that have all the criteria of holding large fish. That's what I was doing on Father's Day, 1973, when I caught the North Carolina record brown trout.

On this occasion, my wife and I had been out of town visiting our fathers. As we returned, we crossed the Davidson River just outside of our hometown of Brevard. When I noticed the river was high and discolored, I gave my wife the scariest three mile ride to our house she has ever taken. I quickly got out of the car, grabbed my fishing gear and made another rapid trip back to the river. Since it was getting late in the afternoon, I didn't have time to go to the places where I had located large trout. Therefore, I selected a pool close by that I was convinced held a lunker, although I had never seen or caught a trout in the run.

Chapter Fifteen
Big Trout, Flies and Muddy Water

My tippet was clipped to a section testing approximately seven pounds and I attached a size 4, heavily weighted Bitch Creek that was tied on a 4x long shank hook. On my first cast, a big fish struck. After a lengthy battle, the fish was landed.

Since it was a late Sunday afternoon, there weren't any stores open that had scales to weigh the fish. I wrapped it in damp towels and placed it in the refrigerator. The next morning, the fish measured twenty-seven and one half inches and weighed seven pounds-eleven ounces, breaking the current state record by four ounces. By the way, the state record I broke was formerly held by my brother, Dwight.

Don Ray's North Carolina state record 7 lb. 11 oz., 27 -1/2" trout taken in 1973 on a Bitch Creek Special. Photo courtesy of the Transylvania Times.

Chapter Fifteen
Big Trout, Flies and Muddy Water

Tips for Fishing Flies in Muddy Water

1. Avoid Fishing During Periods of Falling Water and Sunshine

Although the water is rising and food is being washed into the stream after a thunderstorm, trout are often reluctant to feed if the storm is followed by bright sunshine. I can't prove it, but I feel the bright sunlight penetrates the water (although it is discolored), hurting the fish's eyes. This may give the fish the feeling that they are easier to spot and more susceptible to predators. To seek protection, the fish move from feeding lanes to protection areas where feeding becomes secondary.

It is a proven fact that fish move with the fluctuation of the water. Any good bass fisherman will tell you that during rising lake conditions bass move into extremely shallow water, and during falling water conditions they move out to deeper points and hold until conditions stabilize.

One of my fellow teachers was once dove hunting in a corn field along the French Broad River. The river had risen out of its banks a few days earlier and as he hunted, he kept hearing splashing sounds in one of the pools that remained in the field. Upon investigation, he discovered two trout that had been trapped in the pool. One weighed almost five pounds and the other one was thirteen inches long.

I believe that fish can sense when the water is falling and they fear being "high-centered" on dry land, losing their feeling of security as the water gets shallow around them. Therefore, they move to deep water protection, which makes them more difficult to catch on a fly.

2. Expect Soft Strikes

Discolored water makes it difficult for the trout to see your fly. Therefore, the fly must be within inches of the trout's face before he can recognize it as a possible food source. When he recognizes it, he simply opens his mouth and sucks it in. Since the fish does not rush from it's feeding lane, take the fly, then return to the feeding lane, the line very seldom twitches to indicate the strike. Usually, there will be only a slight hesitation as the line is flowing downstream with the current.

Chapter Fifteen
Big Trout, Flies and Muddy Water

The best way to detect strikes is to make extremely short casts and hold all of the fly line, and the majority of the tapered leader, out of the water as you follow the nymph downstream. In doing this, you will feel the trout take the fly, or it will be easier to notice a hesitation in the fly line.

3. Fish Shallow When Water Overflows the Banks

In periods of extremely high water, when the stream has exceeded its banks, the water along the edge of the stream is usually slightly clearer than the main channel. Trout move from the main portion of the stream into these clearer edges not only to avoid the swift, rising water, but to feed on the terrestrials and other food that have been trapped by the rising water.

Once the trout move into the shallow edges in a feeding mood, they are dead ducks, so to speak, for your fly. Since you will not be fishing in deep water, you will not need heavily weighted flies that you normally use with this method of fishing. As a matter of fact, most of the flies I use during these conditions are large, dark colored nymphs without any weight.

4. Suggested Flies

Any large, heavy nymph will take trout during these conditions, but my favorites are size 4 Bitch Creeks, Yuk Bugs, and Wooly Buggers. I prefer the Bitch Creek because of the large rubber legs. The movement of the legs as the fly flows into different currents puts off a slight vibration which helps fish locate it. Also, this additional movement is often the "kicker" that lures the trout into thinking the fly is really alive. Often, I feel the movement of the rubber legs as the fly moves along the bottom convinces the fish that it is really a crawfish, one of the preferred foods of large brown trout.

As you have probably determined by now, the criteria for a fly used in this type of fishing is large, heavily weighted, and black. In low light conditions black can be seen more easily than other colors. That is the reason bass fishermen use black worms and top water plugs when fishing at night. That is also the reason you should use black flies when fishing in discolored water.

To help fish locate my flies easier, I've thought about gluing a glass rattle to the shank of my hook before tying the nymph. Bass fishermen often insert these into plastic worms or jigs, claiming that a lure with a rattle, moving across the bottom, gives off the same sound as a crawfish. Once bass detect the sound, they home in on it and then move in for the kill. If this method can fool a bass, why wouldn't it fool a trout?

In addition, I've thought about spraying my flies with the crawfish formula that is used by many bass fishermen. This might result in an entirely new concept of fishing for trophy trout in discolored water.

Don D. Howell proudly displays a catch taken from North Carolina's South Toe River in 1968.

Chapter Fifteen
Big Trout, Flies
and Muddy Water

Chapter Sixteen

Catching a Ten Pounder

One particular stream in the Great Smoky Mountains has a special pool, and its image is permanently etched into my memory. The water pours in swift at the head and crashes over an extremely large rock, creating a deep shelf. The water then flows under a cut bank on the left before emptying into another pool below.

This pool is special for three reasons. The first was an unforgettable experience which occurred years ago when my son, Kevin, and I were fishing together. As we approached this special pool, we observed a nice brown actively feeding where the water began flowing out of the pool. Kevin presented his fly and immediately the trout struck, bolting downstream as the sting of the hook buried into his jaw. Just as Kevin began moving downstream to fight the trout, I glanced back into the pool and noticed another nice brown cruising. I cast my nymph slightly to the fish's right side. He slowly turned, swam to the fly, and proceeded to suck it into his mouth.

Luckily, my fish confined his battle to the pool. I can just imagine the chaos and confusion that could have occurred if he had decided to fight downstream where Kevin was still battling his trout. Two panic-stricken fish fighting in the same area, tangled lines, and another angler in the way of the battle is not conducive to landing lunker trout. At any rate, the "fish gods" smiled upon us, as we were able to land both fish. Kevin's measured twenty-one and one-quarter inches and mine measured twenty-two inches.

We fish this particular stream regularly, and several years after the incident related above, we returned to the same area. We were walking downstream and decided to check the pool for trout. After observing the pool for quite a long while, we were able to pick out two extremely large trout resting side by side along the bottom. At that time, we thought they were rainbows, but later observations proved them to be browns.

Since we knew two large trout were located in the pool, we spent hours observing, as well as fishing for, these trout. We learned that the fish moved into approximately two feet of water in the lower portion of the pool when feeding, and on several occasions they appeared to become interested in our nymphs. They would swim or move toward the nymphs as if they were going to strike, but at the last instant they would turn away, recognizing the fly as a fake. Perhaps they spotted the tippet. Their actions certainly captured our interest and kept our adrenaline flowing.

Chapter Sixteen
Catching a Ten Pounder

In July, 1990, I was on this same stream when a sudden thunderstorm muddied the water. I quickly moved to my special pool, as I suspected the fish would probably be taking advantage of the excess food that was being delivered by the high water.

After casting numerous times with my heavy Bitch Creek, I finally hooked one of the large fish (see chapter Fifteen for the complete story). As described in that account, the trout fought an unusual battle. She never made long, reel-screaming runs, and she never attempted to go under any obstacles. Her fight was confined to the lower end of the pool, and because of her weight, sheer power and the ability to sull on the bottom, the fight to tire her (which lasted an hour-and-a-half) seemed endless. Finally, the trout tired and turned on her side as I was preparing to net her. As she rolled, the fly dislodged and she slowly swam back into the pool.

I was one tired, disappointed and quite disgusted camper as I left the pool and headed back upstream to meet my son, Kevin, and my brother, Dwight. In addition to the disgust of losing the largest trout of my career, my back and arm ached from the strain of the battle.

As I approached our meeting point somewhat late, I met the others, somewhat worried, walking downstream to check on me. When I explained the reason for my tardiness, they didn't believe my story and even began teasing me about my inability to land a fish within an hour-and-a-half. Of course, they stated that they could have landed Moby Dick in that length of time. Well, to me, this had been Moby Dick - the Moby Dick of all trout, as I had conservatively estimated her weight at between twelve and fourteen pounds.

This was the last encounter I ever had with the monster trout, and she was never spotted again by any of our group. Evidently the long battle killed her, or perhaps she turned nocturnal, never to feed again during the daylight hours. I pray she went nocturnal, as she was much too beautiful to die without an angler having the satisfaction of catching her. Also, if she is still alive, she could help populate this stream with a strong, healthy strain of fish.

Although it has been several years since this incident occurred, I still have difficulty accepting the fact that I lost this fish after such a terrific fight, especially since the fish was whipped to the point of almost being in my net. For several months after losing the fish, I still had dreams about it, and I still have an occasional nightmare about the episode. The one thought that keeps reoccurring is that I could have landed the fish if the battle hadn't been so long. The length of the battle caused the fly to wear a large hole in the fish's mouth, eventually allowing the fly to work loose.

Chapter Sixteen Catching a Ten Pounder

Almost one year to the day of this epic battle (July 10, 1991), I was able to redeem myself slightly by catching the mate to the fish I had lost earlier. On July 9th, I took my wife and kids and set up camp on this stream. Of course, I had an ulterior motive for selecting this site, and couldn't wait until the next morning when I would have another opportunity to fish for the one remaining monster.

Due to the sun's position, my visibility was perfect as I approached the pool. I spotted the fish several yards before reaching the edge of the pool. When I saw her, she was fanning slowly in her favorite feeding lane in the lower portion of the pool.

Since I was already in the stream, I waded ashore, sat down, and began checking my equipment. I replaced my tippet with a fresh section of seven pound Dai-riki tippet material and tested the strength of each knot on my knotted tapered leader. After tying a number eight, weighted sheep fly to my tippet, I was ready.

As I waded into casting position, I began doubting my fishing ability, as well as having flashbacks from previous experiences at this pool. Would the fish show interest but refuse my nymph as she had done so many times in the past? If she strikes, will she be lost at the last minute after yet another tremendous battle? Will she cut my tippet on the sharp rock ledge at the head of the pool? Will I have to chase her downstream?

Although I was plenty nervous, I was finally ready to cast. The sheep fly made a soft "ker-plunk" as it entered the water and began its drift toward the monster. When the nymph drifted to her, she opened her mouth and the sheep fly disappeared.

She fought in a similar manner as her mate had done, confining the battle to the lower portion of the pool and sulling on the bottom to rest. One exception was when she sulled, I was able to move her by throwing rocks in beside her. After forty-five minutes, I slid her into the net head first and eased her onto dry land.

After getting her ashore and measuring her, I couldn't help but have mixed emotions. I was elated that I had accomplished my lifetime goal of catching a thirty-inch brown trout. On the other hand, I was saddened that the two large trout I had spent so many hours pursuing were now gone.

When I was able to get to an official set of scales, she weighed exactly ten pounds. After weighing the fish, Kevin looked at me and said sadly, "I'm glad I'm not in your shoes. You don't have any goals to fish for now. What are you going to do with the rest of your life?" It is true, I probably will never catch a larger trout, but I will always have my memories of this wonderful pool in the Great Smoky Mountains.

Chapter Sixteen
Catching a Ten Pounder

Chapter Seventeen

The Approach

It may not matter what fly you use. It may not matter how perfectly your cast settles on the water. It may not even matter how trout-rich the stream is that you are fishing. None of these may matter - if you haven't approached the trout correctly.

Most anglers realize that wild, native trout spook if they see the angler approaching. That is the reason you see so many fly fishermen in a low, crouching position, slipping along the creek bank like a cat stalking a mouse. What they don't realize is that their clothing often reveals their approach.

White shirts, light khaki vests and other brightly colored clothing stands out like a grasshopper at a flea convention against the lush, green landscape of Southern Appalachian streams.

On large western streams, the angler can get by with brightly colored clothing because he is making longer casts and is not silhouetted against a green background. Because of stream size and vegetation, the southern angler is limited in the length of his cast and often must get very close to his quarry. The only way to approach trout closely is to wear clothing that blends into the surroundings. Olive, forest green, or camouflage are usually the best choices.

My father was an absolute fanatic about dressing to match the environment, and often carried thc thcory one step further. He always felt that a fly fisherman dressed in very dark clothing stood out against a green background as much as a person dressed in light clothing. This seemed like an extreme idea to me, but it's something that he embedded in my head, and I am sure that it has added many trout to my creel over the years.

Hardware that is worn on the outside of the vest, such as yo-yo retrievers, hemostats, nail clippers, and other flashy equipment, often reflect sunlight, revealing the anglers approach. Therefore, flashy equipment should be worn on the inside of the vest or painted flat black.

The greatest challenge in approaching trout is found in long, quiet pools. Waves created by a careless angler make catching a fish in a placid pool almost impossible. Imagine sitting at your dinner table eating a big, juicy steak, and all of a sudden your house begins to shake and tremble. You're going to become frightened, stop eating, and find a safe location. That is exactly the sensation a trout encounters when he's sipping in juicy mayflies and waves created by a careless angler begin to roll over him.

Chapter Seventeen
The Approach

Do not misinterpret what I am saying - trout in placid pools are very catchable. As a matter of fact, still water is probably the most productive portion of the stream. I often refer to still pools as virgin water, as they are very seldom fished correctly.

One of my early fly fishing idols on the Linville River was an expert at fishing still water. He would spend an hour or longer fishing a placid pool, exit the river, walk to the next pool, and begin again. Most fishermen do the opposite, as they fish the shoals and avoid the calm water. This man always said that anybody can catch fish in ripples, and that they see so many flies they can tell what type of hook the fly tier used. The hours spent sitting on the bank watching this man fish those long, still pools resulted in one of my most valuable fishing lessons.

Careless wading has saved the lives of more trout than catch-and-release regulations. Careless or hurried waders not only scare fish by creating waves on the water, but by the sounds they create.

As a young boy, my friends and I visited the “ole swimming hole” every afternoon. One activity we often engaged in was clanging two rocks together underwater to see how far we could hear them. Much to our surprise, the sound carried an extremely long distance. When careless anglers clank rocks or crunch gravel together, the trout experience a similar sensation and become aware that a predator is approaching.

Sloshing noises made by fishermen that don’t pick up their feet, or move their feet softly and slowly, warn trout of their approach. Most bass fishermen realize that fish can hear quite well, and respond to sloshing or splashing sounds on the surface. If just one bass chases a shad to the surface and splashes, he is often followed by his friends that hear the attack on the bait fish. Trout also recognize splashes, but not as a dinner bell. Trout recognize this sensation as an alarm to danger, and scurry for cover.

Chapter Eighteen

Equipment

Rods

Since I am a custom rod builder, customers often request that I build a perfect all-around fly rod for them. Unfortunately, there is no such creature. Stream size, weather and water conditions, and the type of fishing will dictate the type of rod needed.

Probably the nearest thing to the perfect Southern Appalachian fly rod is the eight foot, five weight graphite rod. It has the backbone and length needed to cast and fish heavy nymphs, yet it allows for the delicacy needed to present dry flies to selective or spooky trout. Eight-footers are short enough to be worked in most small and medium-sized streams with brushy areas, yet have the length needed to control the lie when nymph fishing.

As most mechanics realize that an adjustable wrench is not suitable for all automotive repairs, the versatile fly fisherman should realize that one fly rod is not suitable for all trout fishing situations. He should have a wide assortment of rods, ranging from six to ten feet, and capable of carrying lines from three to seven weight.

Most fishermen, when selecting a rod for small brushy streams, choose a six to seven foot rod that carries a two or three weight line. Because they will normally be catching smaller fish, they feel the lighter outfits will be more sporting. While smaller fish are more fun on light tackle, the fisherman often does not consider the casting conditions that will be encountered on brushy streams.

Light lines make delicate presentations because the belly, or heaviest portion of the line, is located toward the middle of the line. For the line to cast effectively, the belly of the line must be loaded onto the rod. To accomplish this, several long back casts are required. On small, brushy streams, room for long back casts are not available. When fishing across conflicting currents, the long rod allows the angler to lift the line off the currents closest to him, allowing for a more natural, drag-free float.

Long rods allow the nymph fisherman to fish the tight line method more effectively. They enable the fisherman to keep the fly in the pocket much longer, allowing the angler to hold the line tight. This enables him to feel many of the strikes. Also, the longer rod allows the fisherman to move more line upon setting the hook, ensuring the nymph is driven firmly into the jaw of the fish.

Chapter Eighteen
Equipment

Traditionally, fishermen who utilize nymphs and wet flies use slow or medium action rods. However, I grew up using fiberglass rods which were traditionally much faster than bamboo or most of the newer graphite rods. Therefore, I prefer using a fast action rod, which surprises most of my fishing friends. Rod action is a personal choice, and the angler should use the one that feels most comfortable. However, small rods that carry four to six weight lines are much easier to cast on small streams. Heavier lines roll-cast much easier and require fewer back casts to load the rod. Heavier lines also shoot the line forward out of the rod much faster and for a longer distance.

Since the introduction of graphite and lightweight rods, one of the most important criteria in choosing a rod has become length. The angler should always use the longest rod that can be fished comfortably. The extra length allows better line control. I would recommend that people just beginning to fly fish start with a slow or medium action rod. With one of these, casting mistakes are much easier to correct or overcome.

Don Ray releasing a 23" rainbow on western North Carolina's Wilson Creek in 1996. Photo by Kevin Howell.

Chapter Eighteen
Equipment

Reels

I've had people tell me that the fly reel is simply a place to store line while fishing. While I do agree with this statement to a point, I do require all my reels to contain certain features.

First of all, the reel must match and balance the rod perfectly. Properly balanced outfits are less tiring to use, and make casting much easier and a good deal more pleasant. To determine proper balance, the angler should place his right index finger in front of his body as if pointing at an object across the room. With the index finger parallel to the floor, the angler should gently place the fly rod, with the reel attached, on the index finger (with the cork grip almost touching the index finger). If the rod remains on top of the finger, and is parallel to the floor, it is properly balanced.

Another necessary feature of the reel is a good drag system. Ninety percent of the trout caught in Southern Appalachian streams are handled without putting the trout on the reel. However, when the occasional lunker is hooked, it is necessary to put the trout on the reel. It is important that the reel contain a smooth drag to protect the tippet.

Drag adjustments are located in several places on different reels. In my opinion, the best location is on the back of the reel. This allows for easy adjustments as the fish is being fought.

I always place backing on my reels, although I've only had one trout in North Carolina get into my backing. The backing helps to fill the reel spool, and as a result, fewer turns of the handle are required when winding in slack line. This is especially helpful when fighting a large trout that suddenly decides to charge toward the angler and slack line must be taken up quickly.

I am often asked why I put the reel on the rod with the handle on the left side. Since I cast and set the hook right-handed, I do not want it to be necessary to change the rod from my right hand to my left in order to wind the reel when I hook a large trout. Enough can go wrong when fighting a large trout without me standing in the middle of the stream trying to figure out how I'm going to change hands in order to wind the reel.

In closing, I have a word of advice for beginning fly fishermen. Always avoid automatic fly reels. True, they are handy and convenient to use, but they were not designed to fight large trout. As the line is pulled off the automatic reel, the spring inside tightens, putting pressure or more drag on the line. When the pressure reaches a certain amount, line will not come off the reel. If a large trout is hooked, and he decides to make a hard run, he will usually tighten the spring until the tippet breaks. Believe me, I speak from experience.

Chapter Eighteen
Equipment

Line

You don't have to spend many hours on the stream before realizing how critical and expensive fly lines are. There are three basic types of floating fly line available today: the double taper, weight forward, and level line.

The double taper is the best all-around line for the Southern Appalachian region because it loads quicker, and is easier to roll cast. Additionally, it can be reversed after a few seasons and fished on the other end, thus reducing the cost of fly line.

The weight forward is designed for distance casting or casting into the wind. The disadvantages are that you need a lot of line to load the rod, and you can only use one end.

The level line is usually the least expensive of the three. However, it has several disadvantages. The level line is not tapered, which hinders a graceful presentation. They also do not cast long distances easily.

Regardless of the fly line you use, all modern fly lines are a vast improvement over line used just a few years ago, and can provide many hours of fishing. A fly line is not indestructible, but the life of the line can be increased dramatically with a little tender loving care. The first indication that a fly line is about to become useless is the appearance of small cracks in the finish. Cracks occur because the plasticizers in the finish have changed position. Plasticizers are the liquid that holds the solid parts of the finish together.

In addition to normal use, the movement of plasticizers can be accelerated by insect repellant, suntan lotions, gasoline, heat, and extended exposure to direct sunlight.

Several steps can be taken to prolong the life of a fly line. The first of these is to keep your fly line clean! Microscopic particles of dirt adhere to the line, causing the floating line to sink. These particles also adhere to the guides and act as an abrasive, which wears the coating off the expensive lines very quickly.

Check the guides and guard areas on reels frequently for worn or sharp areas. These sharp areas scuff or cut the surface of fly lines. Sharp areas can be quickly detected by pulling a small section of panty hose or nylon stockings through the guides. If sharp areas are present, the panty hose will quickly fray.

Some manufacturers recommend cleaning the line by washing with mild detergent and wiping with a clean dry cloth. Actually, I carry this method one step further. After gently washing and drying the line, I spray it with Son-of-a-Gun vinyl protectant. Since fly line contains the same plasticizers as vinyl dashboards on modern cars, the protectant will protect the line in the same manner as it does on cars. By using this method, I can add one hundred to one hundred and fifty hours of fishing time to the life of my line.

In addition, each time I start to fish, I rub the line with the felt cleaner pod provided by the manufacturer. This not only cleans and waterproofs the line, but it also adds lubrication, which helps prevent particles on the guides from wearing the line.

Chapter Eighteen
Equipment

Leaders

One of the most important tools used in making a good presentation or cast is the tapered leader. Improperly balanced leaders with a soft butt section, or leaders that are not the proper length, will not allow the fly to turn over properly and settle on the water as a natural insect would.

Tapered leaders are available in seven-and-one-half, nine, and twelve foot lengths. They are also available in three basic styles: knotless monofilament, knotted (hand-tied) monofilament, and braided nylon. The hand-tied nine-footer is probably the best all-around leader for Southern Appalachian fishing. Seven-and-one-half foot leaders are primarily used on very small brushy streams, and on rods under eight feet in length. Leaders over nine feet are difficult to cast in our brushy streams, and strikes are more difficult to detect when nymph fishing.

When drifting downstream, leaders longer than nine feet develop more slack than short leaders. If the angler is nymph fishing and watching the end of the fly line, he will not detect strikes, because even though the trout will jerk the slack out of the leader, the fly line will not move, hesitate, or twitch.

If conditions force me to use long leaders while nymph fishing, I overcome this problem by rubbing fly line dressing on my leader. This dressing aids the leader in floating. I then watch the leader where it enters the water to detect strikes, rather than watching the fly line.

Braided leaders offer quick replacement of tippet with loop connections and a long life of fishing time. These two strengths are far outweighed by their weaknesses. A major drawback is the use of loop connections. While they provide an easy connection, the loop does not travel through the guides well. Loops also cause your leader to lose the energy transmitted to it from your line. Braided leaders also tend to absorb water and begin to sink after a period of time. In addition, most are dark-colored, making them difficult for both trout and anglers to see on the water, especially if you are nymph fishing.

Knotless leaders, while being the least expensive and the most readily available, have weaknesses of their own. They tend to be very supple, and while this is permissible for small dries, the problem lies in rolling over large dry flies and any nymph above a size 12. Also, when anglers break the tippet, it is total guesswork as to what size to re-tie back on before tying on your tippet. This results in a loss of energy in the leader and ends in the notorious "pile cast." Some knotless leaders seem to be weakened by the tapering process itself.

While hand-tied leaders are more expensive than their knotless counterparts, they can be rebuilt, which adds to their longevity. The extra stiffness of the knotted leader allows the angler to make tighter, more accurate casts, and to turn heavier bugs over, making them land on the water in a manner more acceptable to trout.

Chapter Eighteen
Equipment

Unless you make your own, good quality knotted leaders are difficult to find and are expensive. The best commercially available knotted leader that I have found is Dan Bailey's Hand Tied Dai-Rikki Tapered Leaders, made by Dan Bailey's in Livingston, Montana. The high cost of quality knotted leaders can be offset with a little tender loving care by the angler. If a section becomes frayed or a wind knot forms, the section can be replaced rather than discarding the entire leader. After a leader has been fished awhile, it is a simple matter to replace several of the soft sections, making it like new. As much as I fish, I only use two or three complete leaders per year.

The first three to five butt sections of a quality tapered leader are constructed from hard, heavy monofilament. This heavy monofilament not only carries energy to the tippet, but it also serves as the backbone of the leader. The strong butt sections provide the strength and power to turn flies over, especially big, heavy nymphs and big, fluffy dry flies.

The remaining sections of the leader should be constructed from strong, high quality soft monofilament. When the energy carried by the heavy monofilament hits the soft monofilament, it begins to soften slightly. Each time the energy moves to a smaller diameter section of the monofilament, the energy is reduced until the fly is turned over and lands gently on the water.

After removing a new tapered leader from the package, the angler should check several items to make sure the leader is strong. Most manufacturers soak the sections of the monofilament in water so they will be soft, and the knots can be pulled together tightly. Therefore, the angler should check each separate knot to make sure they are not rotten. In addition, the tippet should be tested for strength.

The hard monofilament in the butt of a tapered leader has memory. In other words, the leader retains the shape that it has been stored in for a period of time. When the leader is removed from the manufacturers package or the angler's reel, it will remain curly. To remove this curl, the angler should pull the leader across a section of rubber innertube several times. Pulling the leader across the rubber generates heat, causing the molecules to move and straighten the leader.

Several things can be done to ensure a proper leader set up. Placing a twelve to fifteen inch section of hard sixty pound monofilament between the fly line and the tapered leader ensures that the energy created by making false casts is transmitted from the fly line into the tapered leader. This energy is transferred through the leader and into the tippet, causing the fly to roll over and settle on the water properly. If the energy is not transferred to the tippet, it acts like a soft noodle, falling into the water before the cast is completed. When the unenergized tippet falls onto the water, it will usually fall in a pile with the fly landing on top. Most insects do not drift downstream sitting in a heaping pile of monofilament.

For convenience in attaching leaders to fly line, most manufacturers tie a loop at the end of the first butt section. This loop should never be used to connect the fly line and the leader. The loop does not slide through the guides easily, and kills the energy that moves from fly line to leader. This makes effective casts difficult. Always use a nail knot when attaching leaders to fly line.

With a little doctoring, the nail knot can serve as a strike indicator for nymph fishing. My brother wrapped his nail knots with red winding thread and coated the wraps several times with head cement. When using nymphs, he would watch the red knot. If it stopped, twitched, or paused during the drift, he would immediately set the hook. Coating the knot with fly head cement also makes the knot smoother, allowing it to slide through the guides much easier than knots that have not been coated.

The tapered leader is one of the most important factors in fly fishing. Hopefully, the above suggestions will help increase your casting accuracy and help put more fish in your net.

1967 photograph shows Dwight Howell with a 23-1/2", 5 lb. 8 oz. trout caught near Brevard, North Carolina.

Chapter Eighteen
Equipment

Nets

I gave a sigh of relief as Dwight held the net in the water and the huge trout slowly entered head first. This magnificent fish, which I had tried to catch all season, was my reward for a hard fought thirty-five minute battle.

Dwight lifted the net gently and started wading toward the shore. Just before he reached the safety of the bank, the trout tore through the net, breaking my tippet. The fish was so exhausted from the battle that she lay on her side. Though Dwight grabbed her in the midsection, she wriggled out of his hands and slowly disappeared into the depths of the pool.

This episode began four months earlier when Dwight and I located an extremely large brown trout in a pool right in front of the Davidson River Fish Hatchery. Each trip to the Davidson, we took turns fishing for her. Late one afternoon, we slipped up to the pool, and the big brown was in her feeding lane. Since it was my turn to fish, Dwight watched as I slipped into casting position.

The big trout refused every nymph I presented. Finally, out of sheer desperation, I opened my fly box to select yet another nymph when my eyes fell upon an Atomic-Bomb streamer. I knew the fish wasn't going to take nymphs, so I decided, what the heck, I would try the streamer. On the second strip of the line, the fish rolled and inhaled the fly.

At the time, the Davidson was open to fishing on Saturday, Sunday and Wednesday, and night fishing was not allowed. Since it was quickly becoming dark, and we were afraid of getting a citation for fishing after dark, Dwight ran to the house of the fish hatchery manager. We wanted him to witness the ongoing fight so we would have proof that we weren't fishing at night.

When Dwight returned, I was still battling the large trout. The hatchery manager brought a flashlight and held it for me while I fought the fish over the next twenty minutes. When the trout tired, Dwight borrowed my net, since he didn't have his with him. (Dwight has often told me how relieved he was that the trout had torn through my net instead of his.)

We never determined the exact cause of this tragedy. A hole could have been torn in the net when moving through the brush, or the net could have become rotten, with the fish's teeth starting a rip. Although I had fooled the fish into taking the fly, won the ensuing battle, and even had her in the net, a true trophy was lost due to faulty equipment. This costly lesson has paid big dividends because I am now a fanatic about properly maintained equipment.

Chapter Eighteen
Equipment

Constructing Your Own Net

Since losing the large trout, and before I began constructing my own nets, I always altered the commercial nets I purchased. Being a conservative (or down right stingy) person, I have always been reluctant to pay fifty to two hundred dollars for a net. Therefore, I would go to a discount store and purchase a wooden net frame for approximately twelve dollars. After purchasing the net, I would remove the bag and other accessories and waterproof the frame. Failure to waterproof not only encourages rotting of the wood, but allows water to reach the glue, often causing separation of the wood, and a possible disaster when landing a big fish.

Another important step in constructing a reliable net is to replace the cloth string that holds the bag to the frame with small "dynamite" wire. This wire will not rot, and will support much more weight than the normal string found on commercial nets. Next, I replace the mesh net with the highest quality, most rot-proof net I can obtain. When completed, I have a much more durable landing net than the standard commercial nets available, and at a much lower price.

Tips for Proper Care and Maintenance

Nets often malfunction due to holes being torn in the mesh while the angler is traveling through the brush. To avoid ripping holes in my net, and to make travelling through the brush easier, I place a heavy duty rubber band around the handle of my net. The bottom of the net is then pulled between the rubber band and the handle of the net. This holds the net close to the handle and prevents it from hanging down and catching on obstacles.

Once a fish is hooked and the net is needed, it's relatively simple to tug on the mesh, freeing it from the rubber band. Some anglers have the net attached to the handle, net the fish, and allow the weight of the fish to pull the net free from its secured position. There is always the possibility that the net might not slip out, preventing proper netting. When fighting and netting large trout, the old law always applies: what can go wrong, will go wrong.

Nets should be checked continually for holes in the mesh and cracks in the frame which may have occurred due to falls taken on the stream. Believe me, failure to do so causes horrible nightmares, not to mention the pain you suffer trying to get your body into a position that will allow you to kick you own butt for not maintaining your net properly.

Chapter Eighteen
Equipment

Proper Netting Technique

Regardless of the durability of the net, it can be completely useless if not used correctly. More trophy trout are lost at the net than any other time during the battle. Losing a big trout is disappointing, but losing the trout at the last second due to poor netting technique is unforgivable.

One of the most common mistakes is trying to net the fish while he is too fresh. It is difficult to be patient when the trophy of a lifetime is swimming around on the end of the fly line. Most anglers adopt the strategy that they would rather play with the fish on the bank than in the water.

If the fish is worked into netting range too quickly, he will make the hardest run of the entire fight once he spots the angler and the movement involved with the netting process. Once the trout bolts, the angler has two choices. He can either lock down on the fly line in an effort to turn the fish (which can result in a broken tippet), or he can allow the fish to make the run (which usually allows the fish to reach cover). Both situations usually end in disappointment.

In order to get the trout into netting range, the angler must work a portion of the tapered leader through the guides. Once the leader has been worked into the guides, it becomes a tragedy waiting to happen. If the trout bolts, the knots in a tapered leader, or the knot joining the leader and the fly line, often catch on the guides, causing the tippet to break.

Once I hook a trout that I want to net, I play him until he is ultra tired, turns on his side slightly, and I can move him with a small amount of pressure applied to the rod. When the trout becomes this tired, I work him into shallow water. This allows the angler more mobility. If the netting process requires a change in position, it is much easier to move in ankle to knee-deep water than waist or chest-deep water. Also, working the fish into shallow water will not require as much leader to be worked into the guides, thus lessening the possibility of knots catching on the guides if the fish bolts.

Let's expand for a moment on that last statement. If an angler is standing in waist-deep water and holding his rod in the one o'clock position, the trout must be at the angler's waist level before netting can be completed. If the angler is standing in ankle-deep water holding his rod at the one o'clock position, the trout must be at the angler's ankle level before the netting can be completed. Common sense will tell you that a trout located at waist level is much closer to the reel than a fish at ankle level. Therefore, in order to maintain a tight line, the angler must work more line and leader onto the reel if the trout is at waist level.

Every knot that is worked into the guides increases the percentage of a broken leader if the trout spooks. Once the fish is tired and worked into shallow water, I place my net into the water and allow the fish to swim slowly head-first into the net. By netting the fish head-first, the possibility of him jumping out of the net has been completely eliminated. The natural reaction of a freshly netted fish is to flop. If the fish has been netted tail-first and tries to flop, the leverage of the tail against the bottom of the net will often cause the fish to "pop" or jump out of the net.

After the fish enters the net, I lift up, but never entirely out of the water. Rather than lifting from the water, I slide the fish across the surface until I reach the shore. Then I quickly, but gently, lift the fish onto land. Sliding the fish along the surface prevents placing the pressure of the fish's weight on the mesh and frame, allowing the water to help support the load while the fish is being moved to shore. This eliminates many of the problems that could occur due to problems with the net that have been undetected by the angler.

Chapter Eighteen
Equipment

Chapter Nineteen

Closing Remarks from Don Howell

Due to three horrible battles with colon cancer, it has taken me five years to complete this book. As a matter of fact, a large portion of this project was written in Mexico while I was taking treatments and fighting for my life.

Without the insistence of my family, this book would never have been completed. Their insistence was not because they wanted me to write a book, but because they felt I had ideas and knowledge that should be shared with other fishermen. I truly hope that you have gained some ideas that will help you become a better fishermen. I praise God for my family, for the knowledge I have been able to share in this book, and for giving me the time to complete this project.

As I stated at the beginning of this book, God does smile upon a chosen few. Fly fishermen are definitely among the chosen, and we need to take time to honor Him for his greatness.

The next time you catch a native trout, sit down and look closely at the trout. It won't take you long to realize that only God could create such a beautiful creature. A silent "thank-you" to Him would be appreciated.

Fly fishing is not about catching lots of trout, or just about big trout. Fly fishing is about enjoying God's gifts of solitude, pure water, beautiful days and natural surroundings. These are God's gift to us, and we should cherish and protect them as we would gifts from any of our loved ones.

After a silent "thanks", gently slip the trout back into the water and let him swim away. Our children and grandchildren should have the privilege of catching a trout also. A trout is too valuable of a resource to catch once and kill.

- Don Howell
December 12, 1997

Chapter Nineteen
Closing Remarks

Closing Remarks from Kevin Howell

With my father's passing at age 54 on April 17, 1998, it was a very poignant reminder of how life is like the fading flame of a candle being blown out by the wind, never truly knowing how far away darkness is.

His passing was not only a loss to his family and myself, but to the fly fishing community around the world. I think one of his friends, Sandy Schenck, summed up my father's life best when he related the following story a few short weeks after his death.

While Sandy had been in Europe a few summers ago, he was traveling down the road and came upon a small fly shop advertising a master salmon fly tier, Sir Arthur Oglesby. Sir Arthur was a renowned fisherman who had been knighted by the queen. Being as curious as we all would be, he stopped and entered. It was quickly noted by the locals that he was from the states.

Fearing the worst, Sandy headed for the door when he was stopped by an older gentleman, who turned out to be Sir Arthur. The gentleman proceeded with the usual pleasantries, then asked Sandy where he was from. Sandy replied that he was from North Carolina, and the gentleman immediately asked if Sandy knew my father. When he replied yes, the gentleman began talking about his experiences with my father, and began to show Sandy some of my father's flies that he owned.

Everyone who knew my father agreed that they had never met anyone as willing to teach the sport to others, and at the same time so eager to learn from others.

I sincerely hope that in reading this book you have gained some useful information. I remember vividly my last fishing trip with my father on a cold and rainy October morning. That day I watched him catch fish after fish as we worked our way up the river. I am so very thankful for the way he gave his time to teach me how to fish and tie flies. If he had not taught me as well as he did, I would not have had the knowledge to finish the uncompleted portions of this book, or have been able to tie the flies for the photographic plates contained in this publication.

In closing, I would like to leave you with several thoughts of my father's that I think about daily, especially with the turmoil that society is in today. My father always said, "If you hunt and fish with your children, you will never have to hunt for your children." In my twenty-eight years of life, I can never remember

Chapter Nineteen
Closing Remarks

my father having to look for any of his children.

The other quote I remember from that cold and rainy morning we went fishing: "When the day comes that you can not appreciate the beauty and solitude of fly fishing, regardless of what you catch, then it's time to stop fly fishing."

I would like to thank my mother, Margaret, and my wife, Mellissa for giving my father and myself the time to fish and enjoy spending time together on the stream. The one other person who deserves special thanks in this book is my friend and fishing buddy, John Brinkley, for his long hours of art work.

Good fishing,
Kevin Howell, October 1998

John Brinkley with a 23" brown taken on a Kevin's Stonefly, May 1998.

Chapter Nineteen
Notes

Notes

Notes

Other publications from...

FERN CREEK PRESS

The Chattooga Wild and Scenic River, 3rd edition. Excellent all-around guide to whitewater canoeing, kayaking, hiking and camping on the incomparable Chattooga River. Details the river from its headwaters near Cashiers, NC, to Lake Tugalo. 132 pgs, 5.5" x 8.5". Maps, photos. $9.95.

Waterfalls of the Southern Appalachians, 3rd edition. Very popular guide to over 150 magnificent mountain cascades. Includes waterfalls in the mountainous sections of Georgia, South Carolina, North Carolina and the Smokey Mountains. Over 25,000 sold! 160 pgs, 5.5" x 8.5". Complete directions, maps and photos. $9.95 ppd.

The Highlands-Cashiers Outdoors Companion, features over 30 natural attractions in the scenic region stretching from Highlands to Cashiers to Sapphire, NC. A favorite! Newly revised, 80 pgs, 5.5" x 8.5". Complete maps and photos. $7.95.

The Rabun County Outdoors Companion, voted one of the 100 most beautiful counties in America by *Outside* magazine, come explore the mountains, rivers and streams of this scenic area. Contains recreational information on state parks, hiking trails, lakes, camping areas, and much more. 112 pgs, 5.5" x 8.5". Complete maps and photos. $7.95.

The Tallulah Falls Railroad - A Photographic Remembrance, A collection of photographic images and historical background detailing the famous Tallulah Falls shortline, which ran from Cornelia, GA, to Franklin, NC, from 1898 to 1961. Features over 120 photos, many previously unpublished. 64 pgs, 8.5" x 11". $11.95.

Yesterday's Rabun, A look back at the history of scenic Rabun County as told by over 170 classic photographic images. 9" x 6", 116 pages. $11.95.

Biking the Trails of Rabun, A collection of 30 exciting biking trips in beautiful Rabun County. Also features a great deal of general information on mountain biking, equipment, etc. 190 pgs, 5.5" x 8.5". Complete maps and photos. $9.95.

to receive any of these publications, send check or money order along with $1.00 shipping (GA residents add 7% sales tax) to:

Fern Creek Press
PO Box 1322
Clayton, GA 30525

for additional information, visit our website at: www.rabun.net/boyd
or call (706) 782-5379